Choice Scrap Quilts

Bonnie Leman with the editors and designers of *Quilter's Newsletter Magazine*

Leman Publications Inc.

CREDITS AND ACKNOWLEDGMENTS

This book is a collaborative effort of the editors and designers of *QUILTER'S NEWSLETTER MAGAZINE*. We combined our time, talents, experience, and our enthusiastic fondness for playing with a giant assortment of fabrics and tried to bring together as many helps as possible for other quiltmakers who want to enjoy the exciting possibilities of multiple-fabric quilts.

We are wholeheartedly grateful to our associates with *QUILTMAKER* magazine for their participation: Caroline Reardon for her expertise in design and fabric selection during the early stages of the book planning; Marla Gibbs Stefanelli for providing some of the technical drawings; Teri Coffman for her assistance with fabric selection, pattern directions, and yardage specifications.

We thank our co-editors, Cindy Brick and Sara Felton, for giving us a helping hand whenever we asked for it.

We appreciate the help of Madalene Becker, the yardage-figuring whiz at Leman Publications, with the math calculations as we went through our process of triple-checking all the yardage requirements.

We thank computer artist Bonnie Mettler for her contributions to the book layout.

We thank fellow-staffer Donna Nelson for managing the book's production and for accepting the challenge of keeping us on deadline.

And, of course, we thank the quilt designers who allowed us to show their quilts in this book and the stitchers who helped us make the quilts. Their names are in the quilt pattern section. We also thank the many readers of both *QNM* and *QUILTMAKER* who inspired us by so generously sharing their quiltmaking tips and ideas.

...MARY LEMAN AUSTIN, N. KAY JESSE, BONNIE LEMAN, VIVIAN RITTER, MARIE SHIRER, BARBARA SMITH, JEANNIE M. SPEARS

BOOK EDITOR — Bonnie Leman

BOOK DESIGN AND ILLUSTRATIONS — Mary Leman Austin

COVER DESIGN — Kathryn Wagar Wright

PHOTOGRAPHY — COMING UP SUNSHINE: Jerry DeFelice
STAR TWIRLER: Shoshi Ayabe
All other photography by Mellisa Karlin Mahoney

Printed in the USA.
First Edition Printing 1994.
Published by Leman Publications, Inc.
741 Corporate Circle Suite A
Golden, CO 80401-5622
Library of Congress Catalog Card Number: 94-96450
ISBN 0-943721-14-8

Contents

INTRODUCTION

Something strange could happen when you make one of the quilts in this book. Someone might very well say to you, "Gosh, my grandmother made a quilt like that years ago." And, knowing that this book was published in 1994 and that none of the quilts in it is an antique, you might begin to wonder. When the second and third person make similar comments, always with a pleasant smile and a faraway look in their eyes, you could feel the need to pinch yourself and check the year on the calendar.

Rest easy, for there is no need to worry. It is not really strange at all. The comforting appeal of a scrap quilt has always said, "You are welcome here, and we are old friends." With scrap quilts, there is always room for one more: one more fabric, one more pattern, one more good friend to share the fun of making quilts. That appeal, the welcoming attraction that does not stand on ceremony or wait for formal introduction, is the aspect to which your appreciative audience is relating. The joy experienced through the mingling of myriad fabrics is as old and as new as every grandmother–and as quiltmaking itself.

It is true that none of the quilts in this book was made long ago. Each one is a product of the heart and hands of a vibrant quiltmaker who cherishes tradition with an eye toward beautiful innovation. With each of the 20 designs presented in this book, there are countless songs to sing. If you wish, the photographs and patterns can guide you through every note when matching colors and fabrics for a faithful rendering of the original "score."

If you prefer, though, you might choose to let the pattern provide comforting guidance while letting your own melodic variation shine. If the color "key" of an appealing design is not your favorite, transpose the tune to a different hue. The potential combinations of quilt patterns and fabrics presented in this book number in the hundreds. In fact, there are no limits.

Since Bonnie Leman launched *Quilter's Newsletter Magazine* in 1969, most technical aspects of quiltmaking have broadened. For example, many quiltmakers today cheer that a very old invention–the wheel–has taken a new edge in the form of a rotary cutter. What a logical evolution! We might well ask how quiltmakers ever got along without it.

The tools and techniques we use to make a quilt are a matter of choice. Some of us love to breeze through the cutting or piecing or quilting with updated quick methods. Others of us prefer to settle in for the love of slowly sewing. Scrap quilts lend themselves to any and all of it. After more than a quarter century of renewed interest in quiltmaking, nothing has been taken away. Much has been added.

Regardless of favored tools and techniques and the inevitable good-natured comparisons of this one and that, there is one aspect of quiltmaking that delights all of us. Fabric. We can't get enough of it, and never before has there been so much from which to choose. The familiar bumper-sticker slogan, "So much fabric, so little time" has never been truer. It's enough to make our heads, and our sewing rooms, spin.

Tiny prints, large florals, geometrics, plaids, stripes, metallics, and far more. Solid-color fabrics, hand-dyed marbles, and tone-on-tone cottons. Every color of the rainbow plus a good many that Noah never saw. And there is no indication that the fabric manufacturers are going away on a vacation. Add all this new fabric to the stashes we have been collecting for up to 25 years or longer, and that is a considerable amount.

So it seems that the time for scrap quilts has come–again. As endearing and fresh as they are in the mid 1990s, we can recall that the melody is not brand new. Quilt historians tell us that the first scrap quilts likely appeared in the United States in the mid-18th century. Fabric was scarce in those long-ago years, and it was used carefully to make medallion-style quilts. Truth to tell, colonial and pioneer women had few scraps.

The Industrial Revolution of the mid-19th century caused fundamental changes and created countless opportunities for people from every walk of life. As textile production moved out of the home and into the factory, cotton fabric became abundant. The quilt found its favored medium, and quiltmaking soared. The invention and patent of the sewing machine about the same time only added to the momentum.

As the 19th century gave way to the 20th, a new wave of scrap quilts emerged. Dark cotton prints with small figures, often navy or dark red, were combined with a white shirting fabric or white solid for simple pieced patterns. Mail-order catalogs from that era help quilt historians today in dating such two-color quilts. Dozens of similar prints might have been combined in a quilt that had a unified overall look with interesting up-close variations in texture. Such a quilt might today be called a "controlled" scrap quilt.

Following World War I, color schemes changed and quilts took on a new look that was light, bright, and full of cheer. Improvements in dye allowed colors as never before, and quilters combined them all in scrap quilts with plain white or off-white to hold the happy jumble together. Fabric was so plentiful and quiltmaking so popular that manufacturers actually targeted the quiltmaker–something new! Although that kind of marketing strategy does not strike us as odd today, we should remember that, until the 1970s, quiltmaking's popularity had periodically crescendoed and faded.

Many people and aspects of life suffered during the Depression of the 1930s, but quiltmaking thrived. The cheery fabrics of the 1920s continued to be popular, and prints appeared on cotton feed sacks. Scraps were treasured. The scrap quilt became a part of life in America. Perhaps it is this era, whether experienced consciously or unconsciously, that causes so many people to

say, "My grandmother (great-grandmother, aunt, mother) made a quilt like that years ago."

During World War II, fabric use was restricted and women took jobs outside the home. Quiltmaking faded. Some people tucked away their scraps; many did not. Scrap quilts were used or packed away, but they were not widely made. Quiltmaking remained quiet for more than two decades. The "business" of quilt supplies and publications virtually ceased to exist.

In 1968, Bonnie Leman found a new use for scraps. Not fabric–yet. Instead, she discovered a scrapbook filled with her mother's old *Kansas City Star* patterns (many from the late 1920s and 1930s that featured scrap quilts). That discovery led to the beginning of a quilt-pattern business, which led to the birth of a new quilting magazine in 1969. The very first issue of *Quilter's Newsletter Magazine* mentioned scrap patterns, scrapbags, and included an advertisement for precut scrap patches. It was a mere shadow of things to come.

The revival of quiltmaking that began to flourish in the early 1970s naturally led to a renewed interest in collecting fabric. Love of fabric is as natural for a quiltmaker as love of sound is for a musician. Among *QNM* staff members as well as thousands and tens of thousands of its readers, the fabric stashes began to grow. And grow. And grow. Collecting fabric became a way of life. This was serious business, and we loved every thread of it.

Stamp collectors do not necessarily enjoy writing letters, but fabric collectors love to make quilts. The urge to combine those fabrics in new and wonderful ways was fueled by the 1976 Bicentennial and a rebirth of interest in all kinds of crafts. Quilt guilds sprang into being, and fabric changed hands even faster.

In 1984, the style of scrap quilts officially came into its own with the first in a continuing series of *QNM* patterns labeled "Scrap Quilts." It was not a big

deal at the time–the concept and the term were long established. But the inpouring of mail from readers asking for "more" was a good indication that we had discovered where all that fabric was piling up.

In 1985, then-*QNM* editor Judy Martin wrote the landmark book *Scrap Quilts*. Quilt designs from that book continue to turn up at quilt shows all around the world. Scrap quilts no longer are limited to American culture; they are now part of every culture around the world. The tie that binds is a strong thread of multi-colored cotton–and silk, wool, or linen, with plenty of polyester for fluffy good measure.

During the 10 years since *QNM* gave scrap quilts the spotlight they so richly deserve, the availability of fabric has grown tremendously. We can buy anything. If prudent money management is called for, the treasured pieces of fabric we acquire are even more precious. Trading patches is a favorite activity for countless quilters. Never before has fabric been so beautiful, so abundant, and so varied. Fabric no longer merely enhances the pieced or appliquéd design of the quilt; it can be the primary design of the quilt if that is what we want.

The time is right for a new book of scrap quilts, to celebrate many wonderful years of quilts and to use up some of that fabric. After designing and making 20 quilts for this book, is our stash any smaller? We'll never tell, but you can probably guess. Suffice it to say we had no trouble coming up with any number of color variations for each quilt, and we are showing as many of them as we could squeeze on the pages.

Assembling this symphony of pattern, color, and fabric has been a joy. We are pleased to share with quiltmakers everywhere our lives and times, our hearts and hands. Won't you join us in this concert? There's always room for one more.

Choice scrap quilts. We know them, and they are our friends. They are the quilts that need no introduction.

. . .Marie Shirer

Working With Scraps

Scrap quilts have always had a lot of appeal because they have a traditional, easy-to-live-with look, and each block offers a new opportunity to combine prints and colors in different ways. Including many fabrics to interpret a quilt design adds richness of color and texture, and using a different color scheme for each block is more exciting for the quiltmaker than repeating the same block over and over. Trying many subtle variations of color offers the fun of making color choices throughout the work.

You can get an idea of what excitement lies in store for you by taking a look at the wonderful quilts patterned in this book. Artists and editors from *Quilter's Newsletter Magazine* and *Quiltmaker* magazine have had a great time choosing the fabrics for these quilts. It isn't important that you find the same fabrics we used. What is important is that you have as much fun as we did when we made our choices.

Accumulating and Sorting Scraps

The phrase "shopping for scraps" just doesn't seem to sound right to some people. They view scraps as leftovers from other projects, and to set out to buy them, even for a scrap quilt, doesn't fit their image of frugality.

Quilters have sound arguments for buying "scraps," though. First of all, many are passionate about fabric, and they buy what they fall in love with whenever they find it. They like to collect fabric because they love it and want it around them. Quiltmakers think it is as valid to collect fabric as it is to collect stamps or baseball caps or vintage cars. Second, quilters often buy more fabric for a specific project than they need, knowing that whatever is left will join other remnants to be used another time. If you save enough scraps for a whole quilt top, you truly have made something from nothing. Third, quiltmakers know that it is important to have a full palette of colors and prints to work with when planning a quilt, just as a painter needs a full palette when

Scrap quilts are clearly an important part of our quiltmaking heritage. There would probably be no quilts as we know them today if it were not for our foremothers' desire to create attractive bedcoverings coupled with their resourcefulness in using materials at hand. However, it may be precisely this use of scrap fabric that is responsible for quiltmaking's failure to be recognized by the world at large as a true art form. Not that the scraps themselves, or their arrangement, lack artfulness. It is the attitude–the idea of making something from nothing, the economy, the utility– that has colored our perception of quilts. When a quilter takes the attitude that "this is just something I threw together from leftover fabric," she is putting the product of her imagination on a level with a make-do piece of household equipment. Those of us for whom quilts are one of the joys of life must work to erase this attitude. Truly, the pleasure that a quilt gives is so much more than a factor of its ingenious economy.

–Elaine Plogman, QNM Issue 164, July/August 1984.

starting a painting.

But what if you are a new quilter or don't have enough fabric saved? Then it is certainly possible to purchase what you need. Scrap packets of 5″ squares, as well as collections of fat quarters (18″ x 22″) and fat eighths (9″ x 22″), are available from quilt shops and mail-order sources.

Another way to accumulate a wide variety of fabrics is to exchange them with other quilters. Quilt groups and guilds often turn scrap exchanges into social events. Fabric exchanges with a theme are fun for any group, and they can even be conducted across the country or across the ocean. Examples of themes that *QNM* editors have come up with include Harvest Time in the Vegetable Garden, 1900 Revisited, Colors You Love to Hate, Ice Cream Parlor, and Home Sweet Home. One way to set up a fabric swap is to appoint a swap leader. Participants send the leader a large enough piece of fabric (that fits the theme) to divide and share with everyone involved. The leader then divides the pieces and returns them to the participants.

Small, informal groups have even been organized around fabric exchanges. Members meet in each others' studios, and the hostess brings out her entire collection, or the portion she wants to share, and shares small pieces.

Keep in mind that it is important to have a wide range of colors and prints in your collection to choose from when you start to make a scrap quilt. Don't limit yourself to fabrics that obviously go together. The most successful fabric choices for any scrap quilt will include a rich blending of contrasts in values, scales of prints, and colors.

It is a good idea to begin the selection process for each quilt by sorting your preliminary fabric choices into piles of light, medium, and dark values. The light values can include both pale and darker pastels. The medium values can range from darkest pastels to light browns and soft grassy greens. The dark values will be the rich shades all the way to black. Some prints will have mixtures of light and dark colors in them. Categorize them by the way they "read" most predominantly. Sometimes it helps to squint a bit and hold the fabric at arm's length to decide whether it reads light, medium, or dark. Don't worry about it if you get some prints in the "wrong" pile. You can always change your mind later when you are selecting specific fabrics for your quilt. Sometimes these little "mistakes" make a quilt sparkle even more.

Then sort out the scales of prints into small, medium, and large. Scale refers to the size of the pattern motifs that range all the way from tiny rosebuds in calico-type prints to large cabbage roses in contemporary prints. This sorting will help you discover if you need to collect more prints for any of the categories to get enough variety for the richly textured effect so typical of a successful scrap quilt.

Another way to sort scraps is by color groups. Depending on the quantity you have, you can divide them into warm (red, yellow, orange, brown) and cool (blue, green, purple) colors, or if you have a lot of scraps, you can sort them by individual colors.

As you are sorting by value, scale, and perhaps by color, you will notice if there are any color families that need to be better represented. (Oops, not enough yellow. Better shop for some more!)

Preparing Scraps

If you plan to wash the quilt you will be making, it is a good idea to first wash all the fabrics that will be in it to avoid shrinking or color bleeding. Before washing and drying fabrics, test each for colorfastness by immersing them one at a time in warm water and gently squeezing several times. If the water remains clear, proceed to the next fabric. If the water discolors, squeeze, rinse, and refill the sink until the color doesn't run. Set aside for another use or discard any fabrics that continue to bleed color, since they'll be a problem in any quilt you make.

Inspired by the spirit of economy prevalent in the olden days when waste of any sort was not to be countenanced, our foremothers saw to it that the smallest remnants of aprons, dresses, shirts, and other things–always homemade–were given another chance. First, these leftovers, tied in small bundles, went into the piecebag; then, when the garments to which they were related were worn beyond further mending, they were pressed and made ready for a new adventure. They had "cutting-bees" as well as "quilting-bees," and everybody brought her quilt patches. These were looked over, sorted, and often a "fair exchange" was made of light pieces for dark and dark for light, when some member of the circle had a superabundance of one or the other.

–Ethel M. McCunn, in Needlecraft Book of Patchwork and Quilting, about 1920. Quoted in QNM Issue 95, October 1977.

Try to test and wash yardage immediately when you bring it home so you won't have to guess whether something you take out of your stash has been washed or not. Wash it with a small amount of mild detergent and a gentle cycle (cool water, cool rinse) in the washing machine. Some quilters clip the corners of fabric when they wash it so they know for certain it has been done. Do not use a fabric-softener sheet in the dryer when you dry the fabric, since it can leave stains that are difficult to get out. Iron the fabric if necessary to get out wrinkles.

Testing and washing the fabrics in purchased scrap packets can be more of a problem, since raveling is likely. We recommend soaking stacks of same-color patches in warm-water baths until the water remains clear. Gently place patches on toweling or white paper towels to dry. Be sure to measure washed patches if you will be using them full-size, since they may shrink.

Storing Scraps

Stories that survive about quilters of old often mention the "rag bag" as a primary source of the fabrics for quilts, and a lot of quilters today probably still collect their sewing scraps in a bag, box, or bin. There are some alternatives, though, that help store scraps in a more organized manner.

Large, shallow, transparent plastic storage boxes designed for sweaters or blankets let you store your scraps mostly flat, reducing the amount of time required to press the folds out before using them. If you decide to store your fabric in clear plastic bags, be sure to leave the top open so the fabric can breathe and moisture will not accumulate.

Many quiltmakers enjoy working in a sewing room where their fabrics are neatly organized *and* readily accessible. Often the best way to store fabric is to incorporate your collection into the "design" of the work room and let it offer nonstop inspiration.

Using the Patterns in This Book

Scrap quilts are fun to make because, probably more than any other kind of quilt, they are expressions of your individuality. The many fabrics used in scrap quilts give you a chance to make numerous color and design choices. The scrap quilts that you make will be unlike those of anyone else.

Pattern Selection

When there are many lovely and colorful choices, the most fun (and difficult!) part of making a quilt may be in choosing *which* pattern to make. As you browse through the pages of this book, no doubt some patterns will be especially appealing to you. When you see one that seems to be calling your name, then by all means consider making it. If you love the pattern, you are likely to spend the time and energy needed to finish it. Love for a project is one of the joys of quiltmaking.

Of the projects given in this book, some are designed for a beginner who is looking for a satisfying quilt that can be easily accomplished. Others are just right for an experienced quiltmaker who is looking for something more challenging, although none of the quilts should be considered "off limits" to anyone. With the helpful tips and detailed instructions given with each pattern, you should be able to complete successfully any of the projects, whatever your quiltmaking experience.

The directions for each pattern explain the steps for that particular quilt, with references to techniques that are described in the General Instructions section. There you will find information to help you make a quilt from the first step of preparing the fabric to adding the final stitches on the binding, including how to miter borders, how to stitch a double-fold binding, and many other techniques. For quilts that require a special technique, such as a corded edging or strip-piecing methods, the directions are included with the pattern.

Altering the Size of the Quilt

You may already know for whom you want to make the quilt and where it will be displayed. If the quilt is to hang on your wall, you know how big that space is. If it is for a favorite niece who has a twin bed, then you know the size of quilt that you need to make. Knowing the best finished size for your quilt is a great first step.

Although at least two quilt-top sizes are given for each pattern in the book, the size that you need may not be given for the quilt you are making. The quilting may "shrink" the finished size of your quilt by a few inches in width and length, so plan your quilt size accordingly. If the pattern you have chosen is not the right size for your needs, there are simple ways of enlarging or reducing your quilt.

All of the patterns in this book are made with repeat blocks. Most are simply set block to block. For these quilts, add more rows of blocks to the width and/or length of the quilt to enlarge the size, or use fewer rows of blocks to reduce it. Since you are using scraps, it is easy to make more blocks as you need them.

Another way to enlarge a quilt is to sew on one or more outer borders, using any fabric that coordinates with the scraps in the quilt. If the quilt is wide enough but too short, add one or two inner borders to the top and bottom edges only, then sew an outer border around all four sides.

An added top inner border

Some of the quilts in this book require blocks to be set a certain way for the design. Autumn Breeze, for instance, has repeating sets of four rotating blocks that form the design. If you wish to change the size of Autumn Breeze, you need to add or subtract rows that are two blocks wide so the design will be symmetrical.

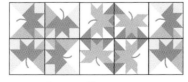

Autumn Breeze wrong

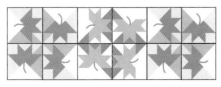

Autumn Breeze right

Give and Take has a design that requires an *even* number of blocks in the

width and length to keep the design centered, so if you wish to enlarge or reduce its size, work with an *even* number of blocks. On the other hand, Calico Mosaic uses light blocks and dark blocks set alternately to form the design. To keep the symmetrical look, use an *odd* number of blocks in both length and width.

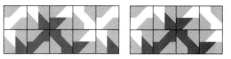

Give and Take wrong   *Give and Take right*

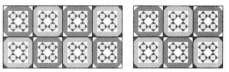

Calico Mosaic wrong   *Calico Mosaic right*

Choosing a Color Scheme

If you love scrap quilts, then you love variety. Scrap quilts can be made with a great variety of randomly selected fabrics that include every color of the color wheel. However, with some planning, a scrap quilt can retain its "scrappiness" and still have a specific color scheme that is pleasing.

Every quilt in this book is shown with an alternate color scheme. Take the time to enjoy the quilts and fabric swatches shown in the color pages. Any of the color schemes can be used for most of the quilt patterns, as well as for quilts made with the extra block patterns in the back of the book. Imagine the fall greens and golds in Autumn Breeze used for Checkpoint. The soft colors of Country Still Life would be charming in Whirlwind. You may come back to the color photographs again and again for inspiration for your future scrap quilts made from any pattern.

Yardage for Scrap Quilts

There is a tradition in quiltmaking of sewing quilts from scraps that have been collected rather than purchased–scraps from used clothing, leftovers from sewing projects, and castoffs from friends and neighbors who know that you sew. These quilts are full of charm and personal memories. Today, even though it may no longer be a matter of necessity to use these found scraps, it is still fun to use a fabric that was once a toddler's romper, or a favorite apron, or a husband's much-loved shirt. All of the quilts in this collection of patterns have

been designed for use with your stash of fabric scraps–whether it is a shelf full of newly purchased, coordinated fat quarters or a grab bag of leftovers.

One advantage of making a scrap quilt is that you can use a great variety of fabrics in small amounts. In these patterns, each design is based on values of the fabrics–lights, mediums, and darks. In a block that calls for light and dark fabrics, any dark fabric will work as long as it is placed in the correct position in the block. So it's okay if you run out of a particular fabric. Just find other fabrics of similar values and continue on your merry way to make a truly one-of-a-kind quilt.

Each pattern has a box giving the yardage required for two quilt sizes. The amounts required for the borders, sashes, binding, and lining have been figured so you'll know just how much you need. Border measurements include 2″ extra length for insurance and are based on the borders being cut lengthwise along the straight of grain and unpieced. To allow you more freedom to use your existing fabric stash, the yardage for the scrap fabrics has been figured more loosely. Specific colors that we used to make the quilts are not necessarily identified. Rather, fabrics are grouped together by value, with yardages for light, medium, and dark scraps given for many of the quilts. The yardage amounts will give you a general idea of how much you will need of each value of fabric.

Finishing Your Scrap Quilt

Scrap quilts offer a great way to show off a collection of pretty fabrics, but the fun doesn't end when the top is finished. Whether you choose to quilt by hand or machine or prefer to tie your quilt, you'll find a "scrapbag" of choices for finishing it.

Because scrap quilts are by nature full of color and pattern, elaborate quilting usually gets lost on the busy prints. Since scrap quilts are often made for everyday use on a bed, you may wish to save your elaborate quilting skills for your heirloom quilts. Therefore, scrap quilts are ideal for tying. This method allows you to finish a scrap quilt quickly. You can use a fat batt so your quilt is soft and fluffy, just right for snuggling under. Several quilts shown in the book are finished with this method, and directions are given in the General Instructions section.

If you want your scrap quilt to be quilted and not tied, you might decide to machine quilt it since the line of stitching made with the machine is more obvious than that made by hand. Outline quilting, in-the-ditch quilting, and simple geometric lines generally look best. If you want to add hand quilting, perhaps you could save it for the motifs quilted inside the patches. To ensure that this hand quilting will show up well, use a solid-color fabric or a print that has a subtle design for these patches.

Borders can be quilted with simple parallel lines or cross-hatching as shown here. "Plaids" made with differently spaced lines fill the borders nicely. Or extend the lines from the block seams into the borders to carry the pattern out to the edge of the quilt.

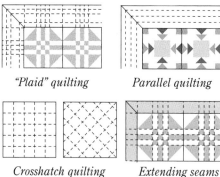

"Plaid" quilting   *Parallel quilting*

Crosshatch quilting   *Extending seams into borders*

Quilting designs for borders of different widths are included with some of the patterns. These designs could be used in the borders of almost any quilt, not just the quilts they were designed for. If the border of your quilt is wider or narrower than the motif, enlarge or reduce the motif on a copy machine to fit.

Other Projects

Many of the patterns in this book can be adapted for other kinds of projects. For example, the appliquéd center block of Country Still Life is large enough to make a lovely pillow. Xanadu's appliqué makes an attractive embellishment on the back of a vest. One block of Coming Up Sunshine makes the perfect-size place mat. Imagine a country-style stoneware plate sitting on the circle of pieced sun rays. The pieced sashes and appliquéd posies in Hearts & Flowers make a delightful edging for the curtains in a child's room. One of the Hearts & Flowers blocks could be used for a doll quilt to teach hand-piecing methods to a child. Three or four Path and Stiles blocks set together length-

wise with a simple border would make a quick-and-easy table runner. These are just a few ideas for using the patterns in this book for projects other than those presented. No doubt you can envision other uses.

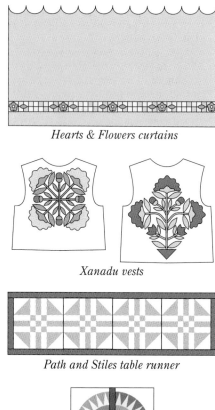

Hearts & Flowers curtains

Xanadu vests

Path and Stiles table runner

Coming Up Sunshine place mat

The extra blocks given in the back of the book can be used in a variety of ways to give you other options for scrappy quilts. Because they are all 12″ blocks, they can be used together in sampler quilts.

Scrap Happy

We make quilts for many reasons–to cover our beds for warmth and our walls for beauty, to give a part of ourselves to a loved one, to fill a creative need, and in the case of scrap quilts, to use up those fabric stashes (and have a reason to buy more). The patterns given in this book are intended to inspire you to make quilts for whatever purposes you have. Look through the photos of quilts until you find one that strikes your fancy. Then pull out those bags and boxes of scraps and start sorting!

General Quiltmaking Instructions

If you are a beginning quiltmaker, you can learn enough basics of quiltmaking in this chapter to enable you to make any quilt in this book.

Even if you are an experienced quilter, you can benefit from reading this chapter. Use it to quickly refresh your knowledge, and perhaps you'll pick up a few new pointers as well.

We've also listed some good quilting references at the end of the chapter that can expand your quiltmaking knowledge beyond the scope of this book.

Words shown in **bold italic type** within this section are defined in a Glossary at the end of this chapter.

Quilt Sizes

Generally, quilt sizes are flexible and adjustable to your design and the planned use for the quilt. The chapter "Using the Patterns in This Book" gives information on adjusting your quilt to the size you need.

Wall Quilts and Toppers

A quilt that will hang on a wall can be any size that fits the space for which it's intended. The average range for a wall quilt for the home is 24″ to 60″ wide by 24″ to 80″ long. Small quilts can also be used in locations other than walls. For instance, a small quilt intended for the wall could also be used as a topper–a quilt used decoratively on the top of a bed over a spread. Shown below are a few ways to position toppers of various sizes.

Using toppers in various ways

Small quilts that are the right size can also come down from the wall to serve as a nap quilt, lap quilt, or throw. Typical sizes for such uses range from about 40″ to 50″ wide by 50″ to 72″ long.

Bed Quilts

Quilts that are intended to be used for warmth can be any size that covers the sleeper(s) adequately. To begin planning the finished size, measure the top of the mattress, or choose one of these standard measurements:

> Twin, 39″ x 75″
> Full, 54″ x 75″
> Queen, 60″ x 80″
> King, 76″ x 80″

Add 24″ to 41″ to the width of the mattress size and 12″ to 31″ to the length, depending on how far you want the quilt to hang down on the sides and bottom. If you want to include a pillow tuck, add more to the length, depending how deep you want your tuck to be.

When planning the size, be aware that the quilting stitches will "shrink" the quilt by up to 6″ in width and length. The larger the quilt, the thicker the batting, and the more quilting it has, the greater the reduction in size overall.

Grain Lines

In quiltmaking, the practice has long been to cut patches with regard to **grain line**. As a rule, patches on the outside edges of each block are cut along either the lengthwise or crosswise grain so that the edges of blocks will not tend to stretch when sewn to one another.

With scrap quilts, grain line is usually not as crucial in patch placement, and it may be difficult to judge without **selvedges** for reference. Many quiltmakers today feel that there is little need to be concerned about grain lines and that the ability to achieve a certain design effect by using different sections of a fabric outweighs any structural advantage that may or may not be gained by adhering to the grain line rule. On the **templates** in this book, we have included arrows to indicate grain line placement as an aid to quiltmakers who feel more comfortable following the grain line rule.

Preparing the Fabric

For instructions regarding preparation of fabric for a scrap quilt, please refer to the chapter called "Working with Scraps."

Making Templates for the Pattern Pieces

We have included **seam allowances** for all the pieced projects and block patterns in the book. Dashed lines indicate seam lines and solid lines indicate cutting lines. Arrows indicate grain line. If you plan to follow the grain line rule, you should align the arrows with either the crosswise or lengthwise grain of the fabric before cutting patches.

From the patterns, you will need to make templates to draw around on your fabric. You can either trace the pattern pieces onto template plastic, or you can trace the lines on paper and affix the tracing to thin cardboard with rubber cement. Before you cut out the templates, decide whether you will be piecing by hand or by machine.

Templates for Hand Piecing

If you will be piecing **by hand**, trace and cut your template on the dashed seam lines, resulting in a template without seam allowances. You will add ¼″ seam allowances by eye when you cut the patches from the fabric. When you piece by hand, you sew directly on the marked seam line, so exact seam allowances are less important.

Template for hand piecing

Templates for Machine Piecing

If you will be piecing **by machine**, trace and cut on the solid pattern piece lines. This will automatically add the necessary ¼″ seam allowances to your template.

Template for machine piecing

Templates for Appliqué

For *appliqué* patches, trace and cut the template directly on the solid line, which is the seam line. No dashed lines appear on these patches. Add ³⁄₁₆″ turn-under allowance when cutting patches.

Template for appliqué

Marking and Cutting Fabric

Nearly all of the pattern pieces in this book are full size. For a few blocks that

will be appliquéd and for a very few patches too large to fit in the book, the background square or patch is shown in a diagram with dimensions provided. The dimensions do not include seam allowances, so be sure to add them when you mark your fabric. Use graph paper and a ruler to enlarge these patterns to the measurements given.

Seam allowances, plus 2″ extra length for insurance, are included in border strip measurements in the quilt specifications. Where it is particularly important for the strip to be an exact size, as when a strip is sewn to a pieced border, seam allowances are included, but the extra 2″ for insurance are not.

> **Tip:** Always make a sample block to test the accuracy of your templates before cutting fabric for the entire quilt.

Ironing your fabric before marking and cutting will make your patches wrinkle-free. Plan to measure, mark, and cut borders first, then the binding. Next, cut larger patches before smaller ones from the same fabric.

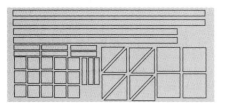

Marking layout

Many blocks are designed so that some patches are mirror images of others. These patches are called "reverses," and they are indicated by an "r" following the patch letter in the cutting requirements and on the pattern pieces. For instance, the cutting requirements might read, "From dark scraps, cut 4 C and 4 Cr." For reverse patches, simply place the template face up on the wrong side of the fabric when marking.

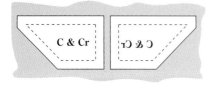

Reversed patch

For Hand Piecing

For patches to be pieced *by hand*, place the appropriate template face down on the wrong side of the fabric and draw around it with a pencil.

Arrange patches close to each other, but leave at least ½″ between patches to allow for ¼″ seam allowances for each patch. Cut out the patches ¼″ outside marked lines, judging the distance by eye.

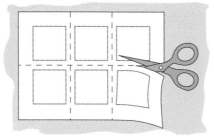

Cutting for hand piecing

For Machine Piecing

For patches to be pieced *by machine*, place the appropriate template face down on the wrong side of the fabric (or face up on the right side of fabric) and draw around it with a pencil. You have already added the seam allowance to your machine-piecing templates, so cut right on the marked lines. You will conserve both fabric and cutting time if adjacent patches share marked lines.

Cutting for machine piecing

For Appliqué

For *appliqué* patches, place the template face up on the right side of the fabric and lightly mark around the template with a sharp pencil. As you mark patches, be sure to leave ⅜″ between patches to allow each patch to have a ³⁄₁₆″ **turn-under allowance**. After cutting appliqué patches, clip into the turn-under allowance on sharp inside curves. Do not clip into or past the seam line.

Cutting for appliqué

Hand Piecing

Place right sides of adjacent patches together so that the marked lines are visible on both sides of the patchwork when sewing. Pin the seam through the marked lines to ensure that your pieces will fit perfectly. Sew the seam on the marked lines with a short running stitch, using a single thread that matches the darker fabric. Start and finish each seam at the seam line (not the edge of the fabric) with two **backstitches**.

When stitching a seam that crosses a previously sewn seam, do not sew the seam allowances down. Instead, hold the seam allowances out of the way and slide your needle through the "intersection" as you continue the line of sewing.

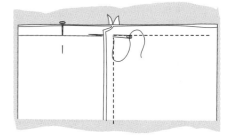

Sewing through an intersection

Machine Piecing

A true ¼″ seam allowance is important in machine piecing, because normally there is no marked sewing line on patches cut from machine-piecing templates. If your machine presser foot is not exactly ¼″ wide, place a piece of masking tape on the throat plate ¼″ from the needle. Don't tape over the **feed dogs**; instead, place the tape in front of the presser foot if necessary to avoid the feed dogs (see figure). When you stitch, align the edges of the patches with the edge of the masking tape. Check frequently to make sure your seam allowances are ¼″ wide. If your machine presser foot is not ¼″ wide and you don't want to or can't use masking tape on your throat plate, you always have the option to measure and mark the sewing line on your patches.

Taping the throat plate

Set your machine for 10 to 12 stitches to the inch. Place right sides of adjacent patches together and stitch an exact ¼″ seam, sewing all the way to the cut edge for most patches, but not for set-in seams or stars. See the next section for the correct way to sew these types of patches.

Special Piecing Techniques

Certain piecing situations need special techniques. Here we describe how to successfully piece curved seams, set-in patches, and stars.

Curved Seams

If you decide to make a quilt that has curved seams, you will find the following extra instructions helpful. Use a dry iron when pressing, as steam will tend to stretch the curved edges.

Hand Piecing Curved Patches

When making templates for hand piecing with curved seams, include matching dots on the seam line on the templates and patches to help in matching pieces. Mark the dots on the wrong side of your templates so you can see them when marking the fabric. Put the dots in the center, at other regular intervals, and especially where seams meet. Place the template right side down on the wrong side of your fabric and draw around the template. Mark the dots on the fabric and cut out the patches, being careful to make the seam allowances even and no wider than ¼″. Pin the two curved patches together at the beginning of the seam line and the first dot (see figure). Sew with the convex curve facing you.

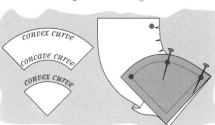

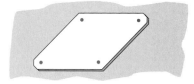

Curved patches for hand piecing, with pins at seam line and first dot, and examples of convex and concave curves

Sew between the pins with small **running stitches**, working the convex curve into the **concave** curve of the bottom patch with your fingers as you sew. Make sure you match the dots on each patch to the dots on adjacent patches by frequently checking the back side of your work and correcting the alignment when necessary. Sew from dot to dot, easing in as you sew, pinning only the section to be sewn next. Lightly press the seam allowances toward the convex curve.

Machine Piecing Curved Patches

If you are machine piecing curved patches, mark the center dot ¼″ in from the fabric edge for each patch and match the dots of adjacent patches. Make small clips in the seam allowances of concave curves to allow easier sewing.

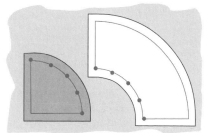

Curved patches with dots

Set-In Patches

Several of the quilts in this book include **set-in patches** as part of their construction. Accuracy is the key to successful piecing of such patches. For machine piecing, mark dots at the points on the template where the seams will meet, and mark the same dots on the fabric patches themselves (see figure). The dots indicate the exact starting and stopping points for set-in seams. For hand piecing, be extra careful to stop stitching precisely at the end of the seam line you have marked around your template. Some quilters like to put a dot at the end of each seam line as a precaution.

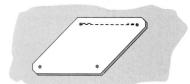

Marking the dots (hand- and machine-piecing templates)

To set in a patch, first join the two patches that form the angle. Begin the line of stitching exactly at the start of the seam line; do not sew from the edge of the patch. Stitch forward a couple of stitches, then backstitch, being careful not to sew beyond your original starting point. Stitch forward to the opposite end of the seam line and backstitch again (see figure).

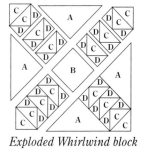

Joining patches with backstitches at ends of seam

BLOCK DIAGRAMS

All the block-piecing diagrams are drawn to clearly show the piecing order of the patches. Part of the block is shown already "sewn" together, while other portions are shown "exploded" to indicate the units that make up the block. When patches are drawn touching, piece those patches together to form a unit. Join all the patches into units, then join units to form larger units. For example, in Whirlwind, sew the smaller D triangles onto the larger C triangles to make small units, then join three

of these units and a C to make one blade of the cross. Sew the center square (B) between two blades to complete the diagonal section. Sew a blade between two triangles (A). Repeat for the remaining blade. Then sew these to the diagonal piece.

To help you see the order of piecing, the spaces between patches and units are changed from narrow to wider. If the space between the patches or units is very narrow, that means that they are pieced together first. If the space is wider, then that

indicates that the units are pieced together later, after other piecing has been completed.

Exploded Whirlwind block

Align the patch to be inserted with one of those already sewn, placing right sides together. The to-be-inserted patch should be on the bottom so you can see the seam that has already been sewn. Stitch from the corner, starting in exactly the same hole from which you started the previous seam (see figure), and backstitch to secure. End the line of sewing exactly at the end of the seam line, not the edge of the patch.

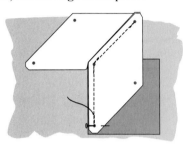

Ending the line of sewing

When you align the patches for the third seam, a fold will form in the first patch (see figure). Again, sew from the exact hole where the other line of stitching ended, backstitching at both ends of the seam.

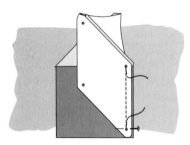

Aligning for the third seam

Stars

Some of the scrap quilts in this book (Cathedral Stars, Circle of Friends) have eight-pointed stars. With such stars, it is important that the piecing be neat and accurately joined. Your star will not lie flat unless the diamond patches fit together perfectly. To join diamonds, place the patches in correct position on a table.

Positioning the diamond patches

Choose two adjacent patches and place them right sides together. Pin through the ends of the seam lines and once or twice along the seam to secure.

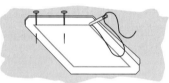

Pinning the patches

Whether you are sewing by hand or by machine, insert your needle directly into the spot where the seam line begins and sew with small stitches to the exact spot where the seam line ends. Do not sew into the seam allowance itself.

Put the third patch in position (with right sides touching) on the second piece, and pin in place. Insert the needle through the beginning of the seam line and precisely through the hole made by the first stitch in the seam just

finished. Join this patch with small stitches.

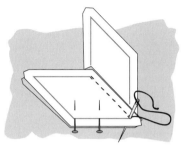

Adding the third patch

Add the fourth patch as you did the third patch, pinning and joining with small stitches. As you add each patch, **finger press** each seam allowance in the same direction. When half of the star is pieced, lay it aside and do the other half in the same way. Finger press the seam allowances in one direction as you did for the first half of the star.

Place the two halves together. Pin at the exact center, the beginning of the seam, and the end of the seam. Stitch the seam, beginning and ending with backstitches as before.

> **Tip:** If you are hand piecing stars and are joining the halves together, when you get to the center where the seam line points touch, do not stitch through the seam allowances. Lift the allowances so they will not get caught with a stitch, and lay them back down flat when you have passed them. Your stitches will go through the exact tip of each diamond, but will not go into any seam allowances.

PINNING

Careful measuring and marking with straight pins will ensure that blocks and seams line up visually. To line up blocks correctly, place blocks right sides together, aligned along the raw edge. Line up matching seams by eye. Insert a straight pin through the seam line on the block facing you (wrong side), and continue the pin through the seam line of the block underneath. Secure the pin by inserting it into the seam allowance, and use pins to secure each set of matching seam lines in the block.

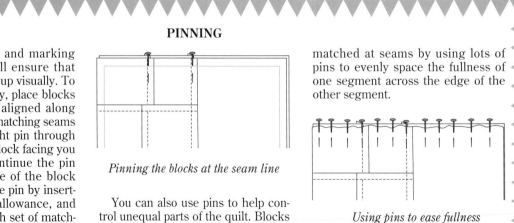

Pinning the blocks at the seam line

You can also use pins to help control unequal parts of the quilt. Blocks of slightly different sizes can be matched at seams by using lots of pins to evenly space the fullness of one segment across the edge of the other segment.

Using pins to ease fullness within a block

When your star is opened up, you will be able to fan all seam allowances freely in one direction (see figure). This reduces any bulk in the center of the star and allows all seam allowances to lie flat.

Fanning the seam allowances

Hand Appliqué

Several of the scrap quilts in this book have at least some appliqué, including Coming Up Sunshine, Country Still Life, Hearts and Flowers, Stephanie's Scrap Garden, and Xanadu. Templates for appliqué do not include turn-under allowances. The standard turn-under allowance is ³⁄₁₆″.

Baste the turn-under allowance in place for each patch. If you are basting into a clipped curve, skip over the clipped area while basting to avoid fraying the clipped allowance. When basting points, trim some of the excess fabric at the point. Then turn down the point, turn under one side and then the other (see figure).

Turning down seam allowance at a point

Refer to your placement diagram and position the appliqué in place. The blind stitch is often used in hand appliqué, and the thread color used in blindstitching generally matches the appliqué patch. Pin the appliqué to the background and blindstitch around the patch, bringing the needle up through the background fabric and barely catching the edge of the appliqué.

Blindstitching

Pull stitches firmly but not too tightly. When appliqué work is finished, remove basting threads carefully and trim away background fabric from underneath the patch.

Quilt Top Assembly

As you complete each block in your quilt top, each block should be **pressed**. Press seam allowances together to one side, not open. Press toward darker fabric whenever possible so that seam allowances will not be visible through a light fabric. If pressing toward a lighter fabric is unavoidable, trim the darker seam allowance so that it is slightly narrower than the lighter one.

Join the blocks in rows with ¼″ seam allowances. Pin carefully so that seams match. Press all allowances in odd-numbered rows in one direction and all allowances in even-numbered rows in the opposite direction.

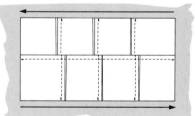

Pressing seam allowances within alternating rows

Join rows, matching seams, in groups of two, then four, and so on, until the quilt top is completed. Press all row seam allowances in one direction, either up or down.

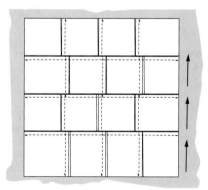

Pressing seam allowances between rows

If sashing will be used, sew a short sashing strip between adjacent blocks in the row. Press all seam allowances toward the sashing strips. Sew long sashing strips between the rows as called for in the quilt assembly directions. As you join the rows, be sure to pin the blocks so that the short sash seams in each row will match up with the seams in the next row.

Borders

The quilts in this book use a variety of borders–pieced, single, or multiple. The quilts with pieced borders have assembly information in the pattern directions (for instance, Autumn Breeze, Calico Mosaic, Cathedral Stars, Stephanie's Scrap Garden, and Tulips and Butterflies). Enough yardage is given for the rest of the quilts to have either butted or **mitered** borders. Instructions for mitered borders follow.

Single Mitered Borders

Fold each border in half crosswise to find the center. Fold the quilt top in half both crosswise and lengthwise to find the center of each side. Then, center a border strip on each side of the quilt top. Pin, baste, and sew with ¼″ seam allowances, beginning and ending at the seam line, not at the outer edge of the fabric. At one corner (on the wrong side), smooth one border over an adjacent one, and draw a diagonal line at a 45-degree angle from the inner seam line to the point where outer edges of two borders cross.

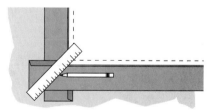

Drawing the diagonal line

Reverse the two borders (the one underneath should now be on top) and again draw a 45-degree diagonal line from inner seam line to the point where the outer edges cross (see figure).

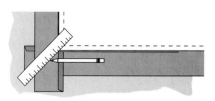

Reversing the borders

Fold the quilt top diagonally so the borders are right sides together, match the marked lines, and stitch. Cut away excess fabric, leaving ¼" seam allowances, and press seam allowances to one side. Repeat at the other three corners of the quilt.

Multiple Mitered Borders

Multiple mitered borders appear in several of the quilts in this book (Blues in the Night, Give and Take, Star Twirler) and are quite simple to do. Fold each border strip in half crosswise to find the center. Match centers, then sew multiple border strips to each other lengthwise. Treat the combined strips as a single border. Sew the borders to the quilt top, then miter the corners as if the borders were made of single strips.

Marking for Quilting

Scrap quilts frequently contain a variety of prints on which elaborate quilting will not show up well. *Outline* quilting or *in-the-ditch* quilting will often be your best bet, in which case, marking will not be needed at all. Such quilting can be done "by eye" or by quilting along the edge of a piece of masking tape. Some of the quilts in this book have quilting motifs designed for certain patches. These motifs can be marked on your quilt top with the marking tool of your choice: sharp pencil, water-soluble marker, or one of the many other marking tools available at your local quilt shop or through a quilting-supplies catalog. Mark dark-colored fabrics with a chalk pencil. Be sure to test markers for removability before marking the entire quilt.

Lining, Layering, and Basting

Make a quilt lining that is about 4" longer and wider than the quilt top. You may have to seam together two or three panels of yard goods. In the patterns we list how many lining panels are needed for each quilt. Remove selvedges first to avoid puckers. Stitch panels together on the long sides, using ¼" seam allowances, to obtain the size lining you need. Press seam allowances open. Seams may run along the length or width of the quilt.

To form the quilt "sandwich," place the lining wrong side up on a large flat surface. Your batting should be the same size as the lining (2" larger on each side than the quilt top).

Gently spread the batting over the lining, making sure that both stay smooth and even. Never pull or stretch batting; just smooth it gently or pat it in place.

All parts of the quilt top–blocks, sashing, and borders–should be well pressed. Place the quilt top, right side up, on top of the batting, centering it so that the amount of excess batting and lining are even on all sides. Smooth the top with your hands. Choose thread or pin basting, as appropriate (see the sections below). After basting, fold the extra 2" of batting and lining over the edge of the quilt top to protect the edges from fraying during quilting. Baste the folded edge down.

Thread Basting

Thread basting is preferable if you will be quilting in a hoop or in your lap. Pin the three layers as necessary to hold them together while basting. Beginning in the center, baste all layers together in an X, then in rows 4" to 6" apart (see figure). Be sure to baste around the edges as well.

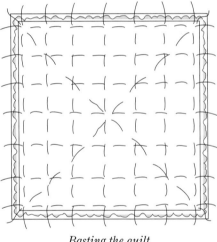

Basting the quilt

Pin Basting

Pin basting is acceptable if you will be tying your quilt or if you will be quilting in a frame, although you may still choose to thread baste. You can pin at 4" or closer intervals, using small brass or nickel-plated safety pins. Be sure to use pins that are guaranteed not to rust, since the pins may be in the quilt for a long time.

Hand Quilting

Hand quilting is done with a short running stitch with a single strand of thread that goes through all three layers. Thread a short needle (8 or 9 *between*) with a single strand of thread about 22" to 24" long. Make a single knot toward the end of the thread. To anchor the stitches, begin in the center of the quilt by inserting the needle into the top of the quilt about ½" away from the place where the first stitch will be. Run the needle under the top and through some of the batting (but not into the lining), and bring the needle up at the spot where the first stitch will begin. Pull the thread through and give a gentle tug to **pop the knot** and tail through the top so they are buried in the batting.

Stitch from the center of the quilt out to the edges so that you can smooth out fullness as you go. Take straight, even stitches that are the same size on the top and bottom of the quilt.

Inserting the needle to begin the quilting stitch

Pushing the needle back up to the surface of the quilt

To end a line of quilting, make a small knot in the thread near the surface of the quilt, take a tiny stitch, pop the knot through the quilt top into the batting, and then slide the needle through the batting for ½". Bring the needle through the quilt top and clip the thread at the surface of the quilt. Remove basting stitches when you finish quilting.

Machine Quilting

Machine quilting is durable and especially useful for quilts that are difficult to hand quilt or will receive heavy use. The hardest part of machine quilting is to learn how to handle the bulk. If

you are quilting a large quilt, you may want to take a table of the same height as your sewing machine bed and place it behind the machine cabinet to support the weight of your quilt. Place another table to the left of the machine cabinet to support the quilt's weight in that direction as well. If the quilt hangs off the table in any direction, the pull on the fabric will interfere with the action of the feed dogs.

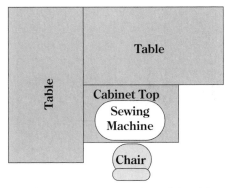

Using tables to support the weight of the quilt when machine quilting

Use your favorite method for marking the design on the quilt, then thread- or pin-baste the quilt sandwich. Roll the quilt inward from two edges like a scroll. You can use bicycle clips (one of quilters' favorite tools) to keep the quilt from unrolling as you work–16 to 20 clips will be needed for a king-size quilt.

When you start machine quilting, you can choose nylon filament (.004 size) or regular sewing thread that is either a neutral color or any color that blends well with the fabrics. As with hand quilting, begin quilting in the center of the quilt. For many quilts and with some sewing machines, it is possible to do straight-line quilting with a regular presser foot if the quilt is well-basted. But if you find that the presser foot is pushing the quilt top ahead of the other layers, you will need to use a walking foot.

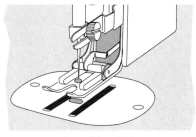

A walking foot

This foot is a special attachment with feed dogs similar to those under the throat plate of the sewing machine. Together, both feed dogs move the layers of fabric evenly beneath the needle.

Smooth the layers in the area around the needle as you sew. Don't push or pull the fabric, which can cause the machine to skip stitches. Pulling the fabric also pulls the needle, interfering with the action of the bobbin. Let the feed dogs do the work. Pay particular attention to the back of the quilt, which can pucker and pleat if not held taut.

When you come to the end of a quilting line, try to stop with your needle in the down position in the fabric, so your quilt won't shift while you reposition your hands or turn the quilt.

To end a line of machine quilting, lock the stitches by making very small, closely spaced stitches for ⅛" or so, then clip the threads.

Types of Quilting

In-the-ditch and outline quilting can be used for both hand and machine quilting, while the stab stitch only applies to hand quilting.

In-the-Ditch Quilting

With both seam allowances of adjacent patches pressed to one side of the seam, stitch closely along the other side of the seam line. The quilting will fall almost in the seam itself (see figure), precisely defining the edges of the patches.

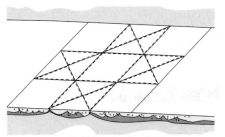

Quilting in-the-ditch

Outline Quilting

Quilt just beyond the edge of the seam allowance a little more than ¼" away from the seam itself, inside the patch (see figure) or along border seams.

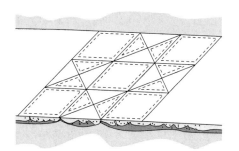

Quilting patch outlines

Stab-Stitch Quilting

Stitch straight up and down, one stitch at a time. Push the needle straight down from the top with one hand, then push it straight up from the bottom with the other hand (see figure). This technique is useful when quilting by hand through the extra thicknesses of seam allowances encountered when quilting lines cross over seams.

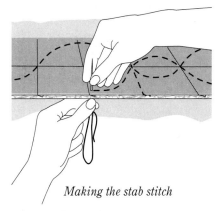

Making the stab stitch

Tying

Scrap quilts often lend themselves well to being tied. We used two different methods to tie several of the quilts in this book. We used both a regular-loft batt (with Calico Mosaic and Circle of Friends) and high-loft batts (with Blues in the Night, Path and Stiles, and Color Twists) to achieve different effects. If you are making a wall-size or smaller-size quilt that won't really be used to keep you warm, you might prefer to use a low-loft batt. For the ties, we used crochet thread, which is easier to work with than most yarn and is less slippery than pearl cotton.

Continuous Tying

Both Path and Stiles and Color Twists were tied with this fast method, which enables you to tie knots as you go without having to cut threads, trim tails, or re-thread the needle until you run out of your cut length of tying yarn or thread.

1. Insert the needle through all layers of the quilt and bring it back up to the surface, leaving a 2″ tail on top. Tie a square knot, as follows: Hold one thread in each hand. Wrap the left thread over the right thread, pull tightly, then wrap the new right thread over the new left thread and tighten the knot. Do *not* cut the thread.

Tying the square knot

2. Bring the needle over to the next tying location. Insert the needle through all layers, and bring it back up to the quilt surface. From the front, slip the needle under the thread that lies between the first knot and the current tie location, forming a loop. Pass the needle over the thread of the loop, as in a buttonhole stitch. Pull the thread tightly to form a knot. Do not cut the thread.

Forming the loop

3. Move the needle to the immediate right of the knot you just formed. Slip the needle from back to front under the thread that lies between the original knot and the knot you just made. Form another loop. Pass the needle under the thread of the loop and pull tightly to form a square knot.

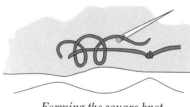

Forming the square knot

4. Bring the needle to the next tying location and repeat Steps 2 and 3, moving from each tying location to the next without cutting the thread. Keep going until you run out of thread. Then cut between stitches to form tails, and trim tails to desired length.

Invisible Tying

Blues in the Night, Calico Mosaic, and Circle of Friends were tied with this method created by Caroline Reardon, which results in a knot without tails or tufts showing on either the front or back of the quilt.

1. Insert the needle through the quilt top into the batting and slide the needle through the batting layer for about 1″, leaving a 1″ tail showing on the quilt top. Bring the needle back up to the surface of the quilt. Insert the needle back into the quilt right next to where the needle exited but do not pull the thread tight. Form a loop. Take a stitch through all layers, maintaining the loop as you do so. Bring the needle back up again to the surface of the quilt.

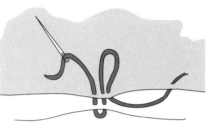

Beginning the knot

2. Bring the needle through the loop from back to front and wrap it around the left part of the loop thread. Aim the needle to go behind the loop, under the thread that runs through the loop from behind, and bring the needle to the right behind the loop.

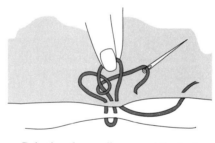

Bringing the needle around the loop

3. Pull on the needle thread to tighten (but not too tight), slipping this part of the knot close to the surface and tightening the quilt sandwich.

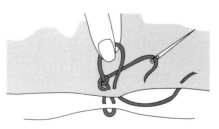

Tightening the knot

4. Bring the needle around from the right behind the loop, and wrap it around the right thread of the loop. Insert the needle into the loop, and bring the needle out to the left rear of the loop.

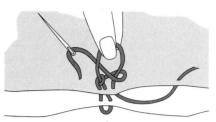

Bringing the needle through the loop

5. With your left hand, hold the needle with its thread to the left of the loop. With your right hand, hold the tail that was formed when you first inserted the needle into the batting (Step 1). Pull both ends tight to form a knot.

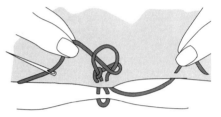

Forming the knot

6. Insert the needle back into the quilt top immediately to the left of the knot you just made and slide it through only the batting layer for about 1″. Bring the needle back up through the quilt top.

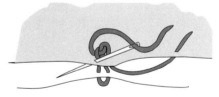

Needle sliding through batting

7. Carefully trim the thread tails at the surface of the quilt at either side of the knot.

Trimming the tails

Finishing

After quilting or tying is complete, prepare the quilt for binding by cutting the lining and batting even with the edge of the quilt top.

Binding

For these scrap quilts, we used a method known as double-fold or double

French binding. Because of the double thickness, it is durable, and many quilters like the plump effect that it gives.

The pattern directions give the amount of fabric needed for binding. Using 2½″-wide strips will provide a ⅜″ finished binding. Cut strips with the straight of grain. Cut enough strips of fabric 2½″ wide to equal the total length of binding.

To determine the length of binding needed, use the following formula:

(Length + width) x 2, + 10″, plus 3″ extra for each binding strip cut = binding length needed

Join the strips end to end at a 45-degree angle, as follows: Overlap the two strips and draw a diagonal line from one corner where the strips cross to the opposite corner.

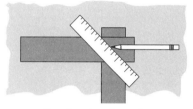

Overlapping the strips

Sew along the diagonal line. Then, measure ¼″ out from the sewing line and mark a line parallel to the sewn line. Trim the excess fabric along that marked line (see figure), and press seam allowances open.

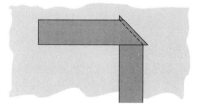

Trimming the seam

Repeat until all the strips have been sewn into one long strip. Fold the strip in half lengthwise, *wrong* sides together, and press.

Align the raw edge of the binding with the raw edge of the quilt top. Start in the middle of a side (not at a corner), and stitch the binding to the quilt through all the layers with a ¼″ seam allowance measured from the edge of the quilt top.

To turn a corner, end stitching ¼″ from raw edge at the corner; backstitch. Cut threads. Fold the strip diagonally at the corner. Finger press fold. Then fold the binding back down so that the raw

edge follows the raw edge of the quilt. Begin stitching again at the top edge and sew the rest of the binding to the quilt.

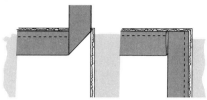

Folding the strip up, then down

Turn the binding over the raw edge to the back of the quilt and blindstitch in place, covering the seam line. Be careful not to let stitches show on the top. Fold the corners to the back. The front will already appear mitered. Fold the back corner into another miter and blindstitch in place.

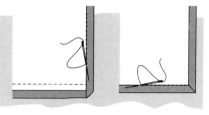

Mitering and blindstitching

To finish the ends of the binding, unfold the free end, fold over ¼″ of one end and use it to overlap the other end by about ½″. Fold binding over the raw edge of the quilt, leaving ⅜″ on top, and hand sew to the back of the quilt with a blind stitch.

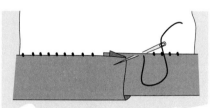

Ending the binding

Adding a Hanging Sleeve

If you are going to hang your quilt on a wall, or if your bed-size quilt will be displayed at a quilt show, you will want to add a hanging sleeve. A sleeve is a tube of fabric sewn to the top of a quilt on the back to accommodate a pole for hanging the quilt. Sleeves can match the lining or can be made of contrasting fabric. The finished tube should measure at least 4″ (made from a 9″-wide strip of fabric with a ½″ seam) if a wooden closet rod or heavy curtain rod will be used. Large quilts will need a sup-

port bracket in the center, so two short sleeves should be sewn side by side with a gap for the bracket.

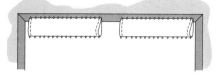

Two short sleeves to accommodate a bracket

After sewing the tube right sides together and turning it inside out, place the tube along the top back side of the quilt (seam side down), pin it to the quilt lining, and blindstitch the tube in place at top and bottom.

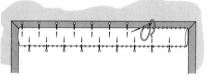

Attaching the hanging sleeve

Signing Your Quilt

On a separate piece of fabric, embroider or use a permanent-ink pen to write your name, date, state, and any other information you wish, such as who the quilt was made for and why. Sew the label to the quilt lining by hand, either with a blind stitch or a decorative embroidery stitch such as a blanket stitch.

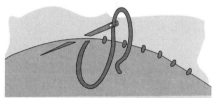

Blind stitch

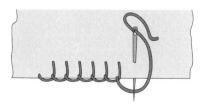

Blanket stitch

Xanadu
designed and made by
Faye Anderson
September, 1993

Completed label

Reading List

If you are new to quiltmaking and need more detailed information about basic quiltmaking instructions, we recommend the following books:

How To Make a Quilt: 25 Easy Lessons for Beginners, by Bonnie Leman and Louise O. Townsend, Leman Publications, 1986.

Patchwork Sampler Legacy Quilt: Intermediate and Advanced Lessons in Patchwork, by Bonnie Leman, Marie Shirer, and Susie Ennis, Leman Publications, 1984.

Home Study Course in Quiltmaking, by Jeannie M. Spears, American Quilter's Society, 1990.

Successful Quilting, by Linda Seward, Rodale Press, 1987.

Quilts! Quilts!! Quilts!!! The Complete Guide to Quiltmaking, by Diana McClun and Laura Nownes, The Quilt Digest Press, 1988.

The Quilter's How-To Dictionary, by Marie Shirer, Leman Publications, 1991.

Quiltmaking Tips and Techniques: Over 1,000 Creative Ideas to Make Your Quiltmaking Quicker, Easier and a Lot More Fun, From 60 Top-Notch Quilters and the Editors of Quilter's Newsletter Magazine, by Jane Townswick, Rodale Press, 1994.

Glossary

Backstitches are stitches sewn on top of each other (for hand piecing) or in reverse over previous stitching (for machine piecing). Backstitching is done to anchor the beginning or end of a seam.

Between is a short needle with a small eye that is used for hand quilting. It is commonly available in sizes 7, 8, 9, 10, and 12. The higher the number, the smaller the needle.

Concave refers to curves that dip in like valleys or the inside of the letter "U."

Convex refers to curves like rainbows or the outside of the letter "O."

Feed dogs are the metal teeth that guide and move fabric under the needle of a sewing machine.

Finger press means to use your fingers to flatten seam allowances or to fold guidelines in fabric. Finger pressing is usually temporary and will be followed by regular pressing when a block is completed.

Grain lines are the lengthwise and crosswise threads that are woven to make fabric.

In-the-ditch quilting is done right next to a seam or around the edges of an appliqué patch on the side without seam allowances.

Ironing involves a back-and-forth motion across fabric to remove wrinkles and is usually done before marking and cutting. See Pressing.

Miter refers to corners formed when two border strips are joined at a 45-degree angle. After joining, trim the excess fabric to leave ¼" seam allowances, and press both allowances to one side (not open).

Outline quilting parallels the seam lines, usually ¼" away. It places the quilting just beyond the area where the extra fabric layers in the seam allowance would make it hard to quilt.

Pop the knot means to bury the knotted end of the quilting thread inside the quilt. For the first stitch on a fresh length of thread, the knot can be popped into the quilt batting by giving the stitch a gentle tug. For the last stitch, make a knot in the thread on the surface of the quilt top and insert the needle back through the exact hole through which it last came. Bring the needle back up through the quilt top, tug gently on the thread, and the knot will pop into the batting.

Pressing involves an up-and-down motion, lifting the iron to move from one position to another, then placing the iron down on the next area and pressing it down firmly. Pressing should remove wrinkles without distorting the edges of a block.

Running stitches are short stitches formed in hand piecing by passing the needle in and out of the fabric along the seam line. Thread color usually matches one or both patches.

Seam allowance is the fabric between the seam line and the cut edge and is not to be confused with the seam, which is the line of stitching that joins patches or other parts of a quilt. Seam allowances in quilting are usually ¼" wide.

Selvedges are the lengthwise woven edges of the fabric from a bolt. Selvedges are more densely woven than the rest of the fabric, causing them to shrink considerably and to be difficult to sew through. They should never be included in border strips or patches.

Set-in patches are those that cannot be joined to the block in one straight seam. Set-in patches are sewn in two steps: First one side of the angled patch or unit is sewn, then the other side.

Templates are the patterns around which sewing lines or cutting lines are marked on the fabric. Templates can be the paper patterns themselves, but more often they are made from see-through plastic. Cardboard and sandpaper can also be used to make temporary templates. Templates for machine piecing include seam allowances; templates for hand piecing do not.

Turn-under allowance is the amount of fabric outside the turn-under line on an appliqué patch, which when folded under smoothly will leave a crisp folded edge in hand appliqué. Turn-under allowances are usually ³⁄₁₆" wide. Machine appliqué patches can be blind-stitched. Alternatively, they can be satin stitched, in which case, turn-under allowances are unnecessary.

Making each block from light and dark scraps of a single color gave this PATH AND STILES QUILT a classic country look. The swatches below suggest an alternate color plan that would give a more contemporary effect by substituting neon-bright colors for all the dark scraps and black-and-white prints for all the light scraps. The pattern is on page 41.

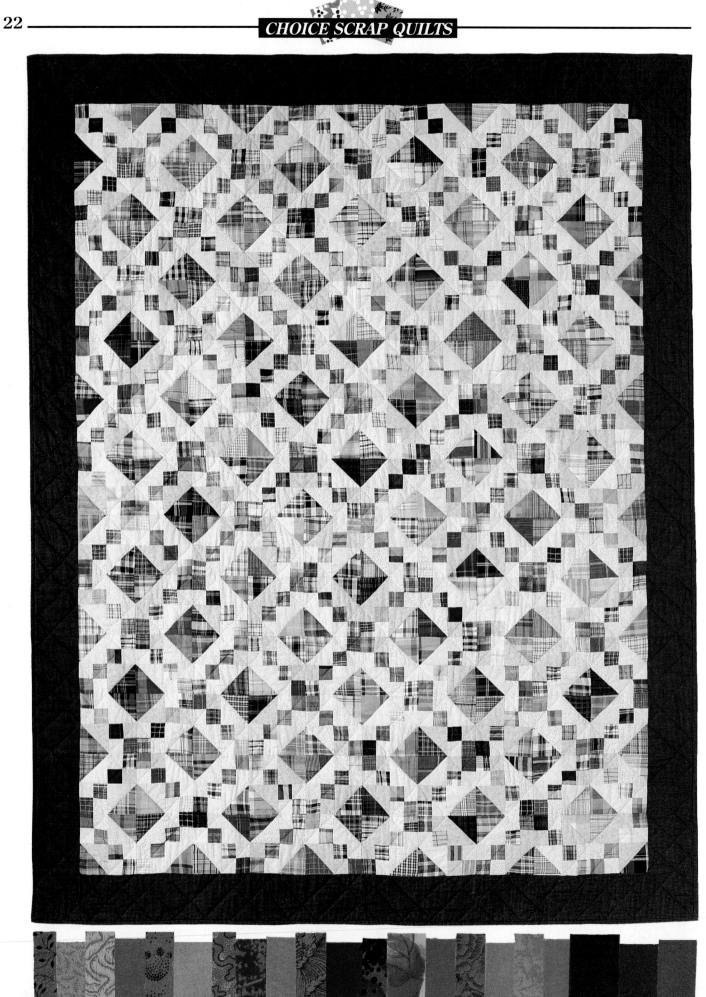

On the opposite page, PLAID PARADE is a showcase for the plaid and check fabrics that are so popular today as well as for those older plaid scraps that didn't seem to work in other quilts. The swatches shown with the quilt offer an alternative color plan, an Amish-quilt look. It can be achieved by using very dark shades of blue and purple for all the background patches, which in our quilt are light scraps, and by substituting clear, bright colors for the dark, multicolor plaid scraps. See page 107 for the pattern.

Above, STAR TWIRLER's color scheme seems to accentuate three design shapes: elongated "football" shapes that form rings around darker "pillow" shapes enclosing light "crosses" with dark center squares. The floral colors in the swatches below would create a more sparkling-jewel effect with the football shapes in dark blue-greens, the pillow shapes in medium greens and yellow-greens, and soft yellow and pale yellow-green scraps forming the crosses. The pattern can be found on page 70.

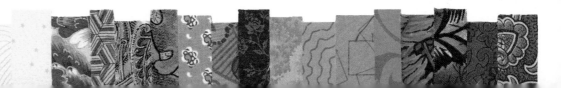

Opposite page, XANADU, by Faye Anderson, is elegant in its rich, dark colors against a contrasting and textured background of soft prints. It would be lovely also, though quite different in feeling, made in pastel print scraps evocative of fabrics from the 1930s, such as those in the swatches. The alternate color schemes shown with each quilt in this section can be substituted for those in many quilts in this book. Or you can use these swatch groupings as starting points when you need color inspiration for other patchwork projects. Turn to page 82 for the pattern.

TULIPS AND BUTTERFLIES, above, would seem to call for the colors of spring in which we made it. But look at the swatches below and imagine it in shades of peach and rust for the tulip blossoms, medium greens for stems and leaves, and brilliant colors for the butterflies–all against a dark blue background. A lighter blue could be used for the inner and outer borders. The name for such a quilt might be Midnight Garden. Reproduction calicoes, such as those in the swatches on the previous page, would also be pretty for this quilt design. See the pattern on page 90.

In the CIRCLE OF FRIENDS QUILT on the opposite page, color families of blue, gold, pink, and green form the interlocking circles of the design. A simpler color plan illustrated by the swatches would be to piece all circles from blue scraps, using light and dark in alternating circles to get the interlocking effect. The stars could be dark and light maroon, alternating light and dark scraps in adjacent diamond patches. Though not shown, purchased muslin yardage or light cream scraps for the background would be pleasing. The pattern is on page 94.

Each block in WHIRLWIND, above, is colored differently to bring out a variety of the many effects possible with this pattern. The result is a rich and delightful patchwork tapestry. If you would prefer to make this quilt in a more controlled palette, the swatches below offer a lovely color scheme of wine, cream, and gold. With as many scraps as you can collect in those three color families, you would still have the fun of making each block one-of-a-kind. However, the overall effect would seem a little more planned and coordinated. See page 102 for the pattern.

Above, CALICO MOSAIC. In this quilt an interesting inter-locking chain pattern is formed because light and dark multi-colored scraps are reversed around the perimeters of adjacent blocks. A two-toned color scheme would also work nicely in this pattern. The swatches below show dark purples and violets with lighter lavenders as an example. You could use lights and darks of your favorite color. The pattern is on page 55.

We named the quilt on the opposite page AUTUMN BREEZE because we chose scraps in fall colors to make it. But leaves can blow in the wind during other times of the year, too, and that suggests other colorations. A brisk spring flurry might tumble leaves in shades of rose against patches of assorted sky blues. Very pale gold scraps could be used for background patches. Turn to page 48 for the pattern.

BLUES IN THE NIGHT on the opposite page uses one of the most popular two-color combinations, blue and white. (Notice, though, that including blue and white prints with other color accents in their print motifs adds richness to the overall texture.) Red and white, green and yellow, or any two colors you like together–one in darks and the other in lights–would work well in this quilt. The swatches offer a more contemporary multicolor approach. We suggest substituting blues, reds, and grays for all the dark and medium patches, and substituting golds and creams for the light patches. The pattern is on page 64.

HEARTS AND FLOWERS, above, is a lively quilt with a country feeling achieved by piecing some of the hearts from dark scraps in unexpected colors such as blue, green, and orange. Reds, whites, and blues would give a more bold folk-art look. Piece all the hearts in red scraps on a background of white and off-white scraps. (The whites are not shown in the swatches below.) Get a checkerboard effect in the sashes between the blocks by alternating squares of dark blue and light blue scraps. To keep the strong effect of this coloration, do not add the appliqué in this version. You will find the pattern on page 61.

Opposite page, SECOND TIME AROUND. This pattern is a particularly versatile one that would be pretty in many colorations. For example, you might want to interpret the chrysanthemum-like flowers as stars by alternating light and dark scraps in pairs of colors in the pointed petal shapes. Another coloration we like is shown in the swatches. The red scraps would go in the flower petals with blue scraps in the flowers' center squares. We suggest scraps of light creams and beiges for the background triangles that are dark green in the quilt shown. For the large squares and inner border, a good choice would be a medium-dark, large-scale print with browns and perhaps a touch of blue in it. An outer border of a dark red print would frame it nicely. The pattern is on page 58.

COUNTRY STILL LIFE, above, would make a delightful accent piece in any room decorated in an informal, comfortable style. Although the design was intended to have a home-spun flavor, it can appear more sophisticated and contemporary in other colors if that style is one you prefer. Look at the swatches below and imagine this color plan. Use a bold black print, such as the one on the right, with a printed muslin for the checkerboard border. Use a wide range of reds, wines, and golds for the appliquéd flowers over a cream background. Select a teal print for the pitcher and a rich brown for the bowl. Scraps of grayed greens or a single gray-green print would work equally well for the stems and leaves. A purple print could be perfect for the two narrow borders with a medium beige and black print for the outer border. You will find the pattern on page 72.

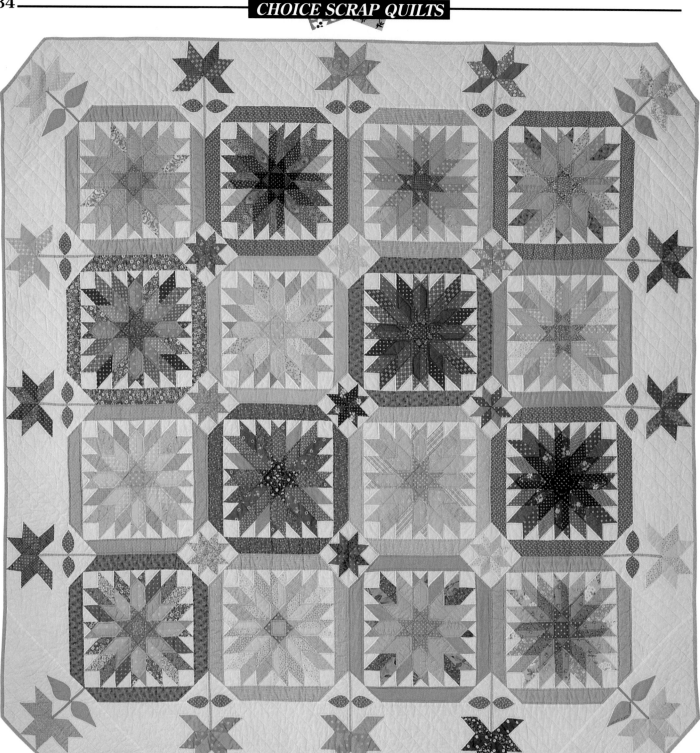

STEPHANIE'S SCRAP GARDEN is so pretty as it is, swatches offering another color plan hardly seem necessary. But envision the quilt in shades of yellow and gold in all the large flowers and in shades of peach and rust for the smaller flowers in the setting squares and border. Shades and tints of teal (not shown) for the leaves and sashes would be lovely over a pale background color of your choice. A warm cream or a white-on-white print would be two colors to consider for the background. The pattern is on page 87.

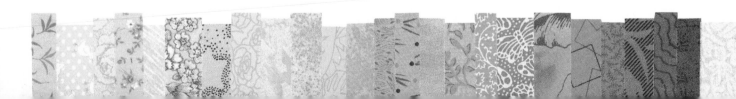

COLUMBIA STAR is an ideal pattern for a scrap quilt, because its design looks wonderful in any assortment of colors. As long as there is the contrast of light and dark values, the stars may be dark and the cube shapes light, as in this quilt, or vice versa. Here, the soft-colored cubes seem to float in front of the rich, dark stars. If you choose the colors in the swatches below and reverse the position of darks and lights, shining stars will advance and twinkle against a night sky of deep shades of blue. See the pattern on page 79.

COMING UP SUNSHINE by Marion Huyck, above, could hardly be improved upon, but it is sure to be a success in any pleasing combination of contrasting colors in lights and darks for each quarter block. The swatches below show some examples of current fabrics that would work well in this quilt. Blue-greens, such as teal, would be nice for stems and leaves. Turn to page 97 to find the pattern.

COLOR TWISTS, shown on the opposite page, could be transformed into a special holiday quilt. All it would take is some additional color twists. Use bright green and dark green scraps to form "wreaths" against a background of very pale prints of green and white. Use a red seasonal stripe and bright red scraps in the corners of the blocks and the same red stripe for the border. Pattern is on page 52.

GIVE AND TAKE looks great in multicolored scraps, but it would be lovely in a more limited palette also. As the swatches below remind us, rose and green are a favorite color combination. You could substitute green scraps for all the dark colors in GIVE AND TAKE, substitute rose scraps for all the medium colors, and keep light scraps in the same position to serve as background. Turn to page 105 for the pattern.

CATHEDRAL STARS is a very dramatic and contemporary-looking quilt in its bright colors combined with black and gray. Imagine how different it would look in the cool colors shown below. Scraps of gold metallic prints could be used in all the stars, and blue scraps could be substituted for the black print. As a background color instead of gray, a soft beige print such as the one on the left would enhance the serene effect. The pattern is on page 44.

CHECKPOINT is a good pattern choice for creative scrap use. The small and large nine-patch blocks offer many coloring opportunities. The swatches suggest one example. For the light and dark scraps of a single color in each block, substitute a controlled palette of rust, tan, cream, and black scraps in the large nine-patch blocks. Replace the red print with a dark blue print and use an off-white print instead of muslin in the small blocks and the setting strips. A soft, gray blue print would work well in the edge triangles. The pattern is on page 67.

Path and Stiles

Adapted from a classic Nancy Cabot design, made by Maria Reardon Capp and Wilma Allen

Many patterns that have been part of quiltmaking history look fresh and new with the use of contemporary prints. Path and Stiles was first presented in a Nancy Cabot syndicated newspaper column in the 1930s. The simple piecing with large triangles and easy strips and squares makes this quilt a good choice for the beginner.

For those of you who enjoy the ease of rotary cutting, this pattern is ideal. We give alternate strip-piecing methods so you can use your rotary cutter and mat to breeze through the cutting and piecing. The boxed directions take you through making the nine-patch and three-strip units. If you have never tried strip-piecing techniques before, this is a good quilt with which to learn.

We've tied this quilt with the continuous tying method described in the General Instructions. If you prefer to hand or machine quilt, the large triangles are just the place to show off your quilting skills. We have included a quilting motif designed for those patches.

The 46½"-square wall quilt is also the perfect size for a baby or crib quilt. The color variation shown in the color pages was chosen with a child in mind.

FULL-SIZE QUILT

Cutting and Sewing the Blocks

1 The medium-print fabrics that are used for the patches are tone-on-tone prints, so they almost look like solids. Larger-scale prints or solids will work just as well in this pattern. Choose two coordinating fabrics for each block.

In the quilt shown, each color combination is used in at least two blocks. For the strip-piecing method, three blocks are made from each color combination. Cut the patches as listed in the materials and cutting box or follow our directions for strip piecing.

2 Referring to the block diagram, make 42 blocks, substituting strip-pieced segments for the A and B patches if you used that technique.

Assembling the Quilt Top

3 Once all of the blocks are made, it is fun to take the time to play with the arrangement before sewing them together. You can plan to have the lightest blocks scattered across the surface, or center them in the middle of the quilt and surround them with the darker blocks. Be careful that you don't put two blocks that are alike too close to one another.

On a large flat surface, arrange the blocks in seven rows of six blocks each. Pick up the blocks in order for each row, and keep these stacks in order as you stitch. Join blocks in rows, pressing the seam allowances in opposite directions for alternating rows. Join the rows, matching the seams. Press the seam allowances between rows in one direction.

4 You can learn how to sew on borders and miter the corners in the General Instructions in this book. Matching centers, sew the border strips to the quilt. Miter the cor[...]

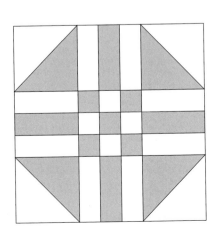

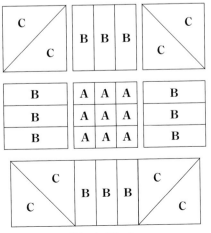

Block Piecing

Block Size: 13½″	Queen-Size Quilt	Wall Quilt
Quilt Size:	90″ x 103½″	46½″ x 46½″
Materials and Cutting:		
Lt. Scraps	**5¼ yds.**	**1⅛ yds.**
	168 A, 336 B, 168 C	36 A, 72 B, 36 C
Med. Scraps	**4 yds.**	**1⅛ yds.**
	210 A, 168 B, 168 C	45 A, 36 B, 36 C
Binding Print	**1 yd.**	**½ yd.**
	2½″ x 11⅜ yds.	2½″ x 5¾ yds.
Border Print	**3⅛ yds.**	**1⅝ yds.**
2 borders	5″ x 106″	3½″ x 49″
2 borders	5″ x 92½″	3½″ x 49″
Lining	**8¼ yds.**	**3 yds.**
3 panels	36⅜″ x 94″	
2 panels		25¾″ x 50½″
Batting	**94″ x 107½″**	**50½″ x 50½″**

and trim the excess to leave ¼″ seam allowances.

Taking It to the Finish

5 Mark the quilting motif in C patches if you are using it. If you plan to use the motif in the border, mark three motifs beside each block, centering the motifs in the border as shown on the diagram. Extend the curved line at the corners as shown. Sew the lining panels together. Layer the quilt lining, batting, and top; baste.

6 Tie the quilt if you prefer. Or quilt the marked motifs in C's and in the border. Quilt in-the-ditch around A and B patches. Apply double-fold binding to finish. Add a label to the back that includes your name, the recipient's name, the date, and the place.

WALL QUILT

1 Only nine blocks are needed for this 46½″ x 46½″ quilt. If you are using the strip-piecing methods, you need to choose three different color combinations. You will make three blocks from each of the combinations. Referring to the block diagram, make nine blocks, substituting the strip-pieced units in place of the A and B patches.

2 Arrange and join the blocks in three rows of three blocks each. Join the rows. Mark the quilting motif in C's. Sew the lining panels together. Layer the quilt lining, batting, and backing, and baste. Follow Step 6 for the full-size quilt to finish, except quilt horizontal and vertical lines spaced 1½″ apart in the borders. If desired, add a 3″-wide sleeve on the back of the quilt along the top edge for hanging with a rod.

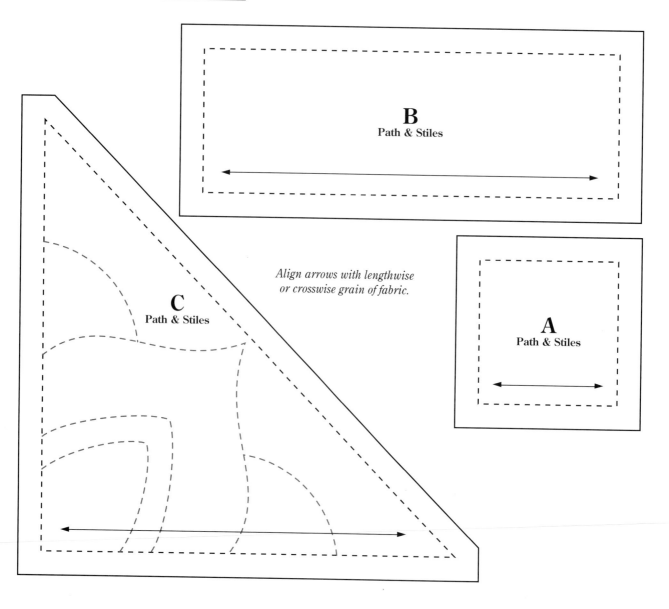

Align arrows with lengthwise or crosswise grain of fabric.

B
Path & Stiles

A
Path & Stiles

C
Path & Stiles

STRIP-PIECING METHODS

The Path and Stiles block has units that are ideal for strip-piecing methods. These units will take the place of the A and B patches in the block. Make three blocks from each of 14 color combinations for the full-size quilt. Make three blocks from each of three color combinations for the wall quilt. Cut the borders, binding, and C patches as listed in the box.

Instead of cutting A and B patches, cut strips for quick piecing as follows: For every three blocks, from ⅓ yard of light print, cut four strips 2″ x 40″ and one strip 2″ x 13″. From ¼ yard of medium print, cut two strips 2″ x 40″ and two strips 2″ x 13″.

Join a 40″ medium strip between two light strips along their long edges to make a band 1. Press the seam allowances toward the medium fabric. Repeat to make two band 1's. Trim the end of the band perpendicular to the seams. From the bands, cut a total of 12 segments, each 5″ wide as shown. (These will take the place of B patches in the blocks.) Also cut a total of three segments each 2″ wide. (These will take the place of the A patches.) Set these aside.

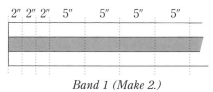

Band 1 (Make 2.)

Join a 13″ light strip between the two medium strips. Press seam allowances toward the medium fabric. This is band 2. From this band, cut six segments each 2″ wide. Set aside.

Band 2 (Make 1.)

Referring to the block diagram, make the center of the block as follows: Sew a 2″ segment from band 1 between two 2″ segments from band 2 to make a checkered center. Repeat to make three centers. (These will take the place of the checkerboard centers made with A patches.)

Make three blocks using the checkered centers, the 5″ pieced segments, and the cut C patches. Repeat with the other color combinations to make a total of 42 blocks for the full-size quilt or nine blocks for the wall quilt.

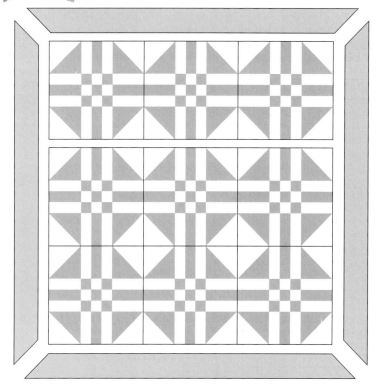

Wall Quilt Assembly

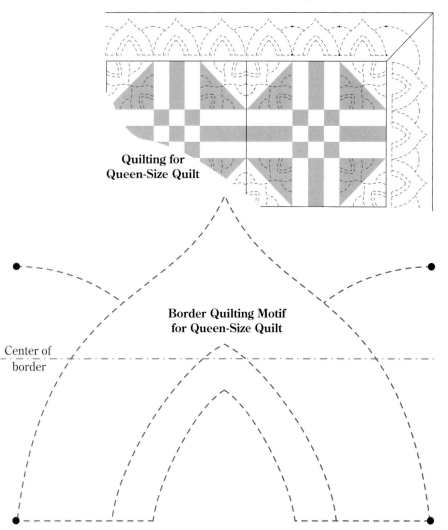

Quilting for Queen-Size Quilt

Border Quilting Motif for Queen-Size Quilt

Center of border

Cathedral Stars

Adapted from a design by Bea Yurkerwich, made by Carolee Miller

Bright, scrappy stars twinkle against a background of two neutrals–a soft gray-and-white print and a sophisticated black-and-white print. The use of these sharply contrasting prints as a setting for the brilliant stars makes the quilt excitingly contemporary in feeling, although it is based on a traditional block. We named it Cathedral Stars because its look reminded us somewhat of stained glass.

This design gives you the perfect chance to use some of your fabric stash that you have sorted into color families. Each star is made of eight patches from the same color family.

Note that the quilting motif we designed for the large side patches will show up to best advantage on a solid fabric or a muted print that reads almost solid, such as the gray-and-white print we chose.

FULL-SIZE QUILT

Making the Blocks

1 Cut patches as listed in the materials and cutting box and stack them in piles by color. Look at the block diagrams. Notice that all three blocks include a star and only the edge patches and color placements vary. To ensure that you get the colors in the correct position, lay out the patches for one block at a time before sewing them together.

These blocks contain some set-in patches. If you want to piece by machine but have no experience with set-in patches, we suggest you try a practice block before starting your quilt. Tips for making it easy to set in patches are in the section on special piecing techniques in the General Instructions.

Referring to the block piecing dia-

grams, make four W blocks, 10 X blocks, 12 Y blocks, and six Z blocks. We suggest you press all the seams in the block in one direction, either clockwise or counterclockwise, as you join the sections of the block. Press each

finished block.

Assembling the Quilt Top

2 Using the quilt assembly diagram on page 47 as a guide, lay out blocks on the floor, a design wall (see

Block W

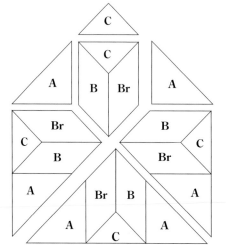

Block W Piecing

Block X

page 46), or a large table so that you can check placement for color balance as you arrange the blocks. Adjust block arrangement as necessary until you have a color balance that pleases you.

3 Working one diagonal row at a time, join the block(s) and E patches to complete the rows. Press the joining seams in each row alternately to the right and to the left so that when the rows are joined the seams that abut go

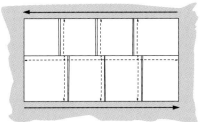

in opposite directions (see figure). Join the rows.

4 Add borders, mitering corners and trimming excess to leave ¼″ seam allowances as explained in the General Instructions. Press the quilt top.

Taking It to the Finish

5 You can quilt in-the-ditch as we did and extend some of the lines into the border as shown in Quilting Diagram II. Or, you may choose to mark the quilting motifs in the background E patches and borders as indicated in Quilting Diagram I. The repeating motif for the border is a single flower and leaf.

To mark the motifs in the border strips, fold the quilt in half and crease each border strip to find the center. Beginning in the center of a long (side) border, mark two motifs facing each other as shown. Working from the center out, align the dot-dash line on the motif with the middle of the border strip. Mark motifs ½″ apart. Add lines connecting motifs. Mark nine motifs going in one direction and nine motifs in the reverse direction along each side border. Similarly, begin in the center of a short (top/bottom) border. Mark two motifs facing each other.

Space motifs ⅝″ apart. Mark 14 motifs along each short border, half in one direction and half in the opposite. Adjust the spacing between the motifs if needed to fit.

6 Sew the lining panels together. Layer the quilt lining, batting, and top as explained in the General Instructions. Thread- or pin-baste the layers together.

7 Quilt motifs in E's and borders as marked, and outline quilt the stars ¼″ from seams. Apply double-fold binding to finish. Don't forget a label to identify your quilt for future generations!

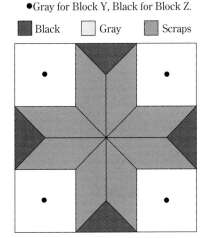

A
Cathedral Stars

Block Size: 12¾″	Full-Size Quilt	Wall Quilt
Quilt Size:	78″ x 96″	60″ x 60″
Quilt Requires:	4 W blocks	4 W blocks
	10 X blocks	4 X blocks
	12 Y blocks	4 Y blocks
	6 Z blocks	1 Z block
Materials and Cutting:		
Bright Scraps	**3 yds.**	**1⅜ yds.**
	128 B, 128 Br	52 B, 52 Br
Gray Print	**2⅝ yds.**	**1¼ yds.**
	46 A, 36 C,	28 A, 24 C,
	48 D, 14 E	16 D, 8 E
Black Print	**3⅞ yds.**	**2 yds.**
2 borders	6½″ x 98½″	6½″ x 62½″
2 borders	6½″ x 80½″	6½″ x 62½″
	28 A, 96 C,	16 A, 32 C,
	34 D	8 D
Red Print	**⅞ yd.**	**⅝ yd.**
binding	2½″ x 10⅝ yds.	2½″ x 7¾ yds.
Lining	**5⅞ yds.**	**3¾ yds.**
2 panels	41¼″ x 100″	32½″ x 64″
Batting	**82″ x 100″**	**64″ x 64″**

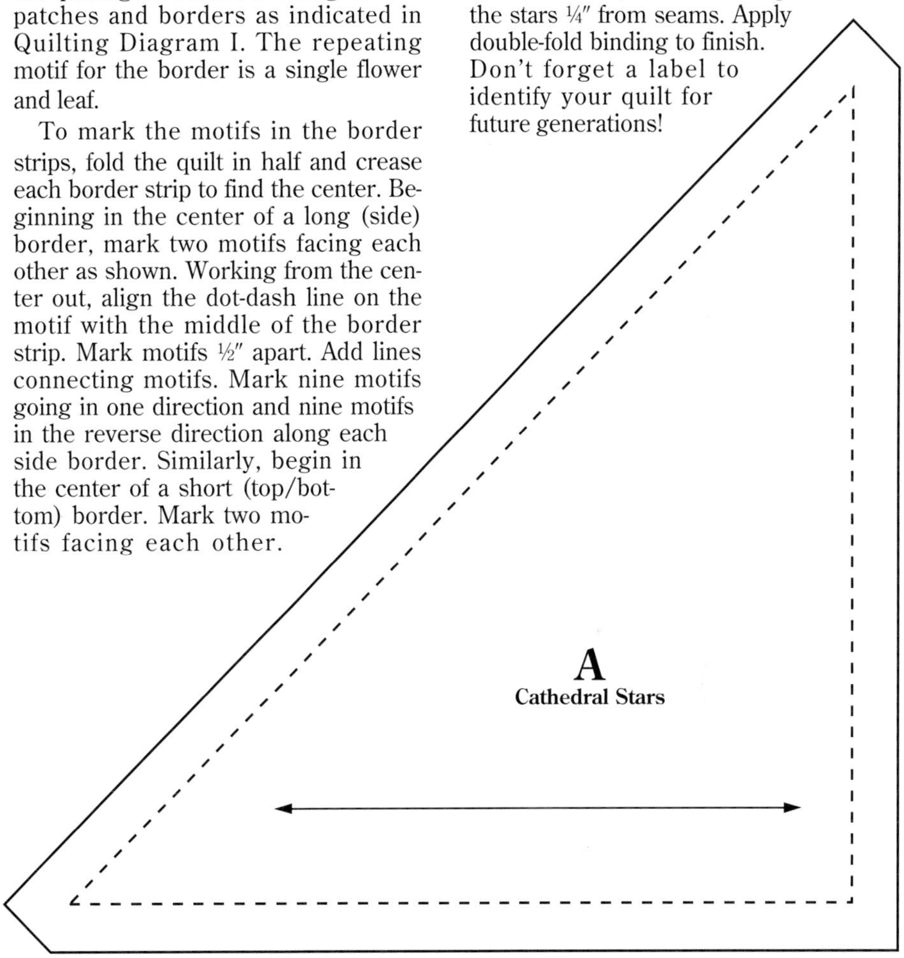

• Gray for Block Y, Black for Block Z.

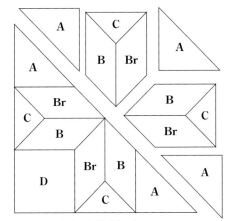

Block X Piecing

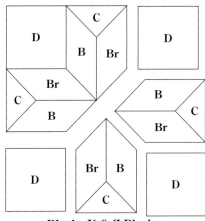

Blocks Y & Z

Blocks Y & Z Piecing

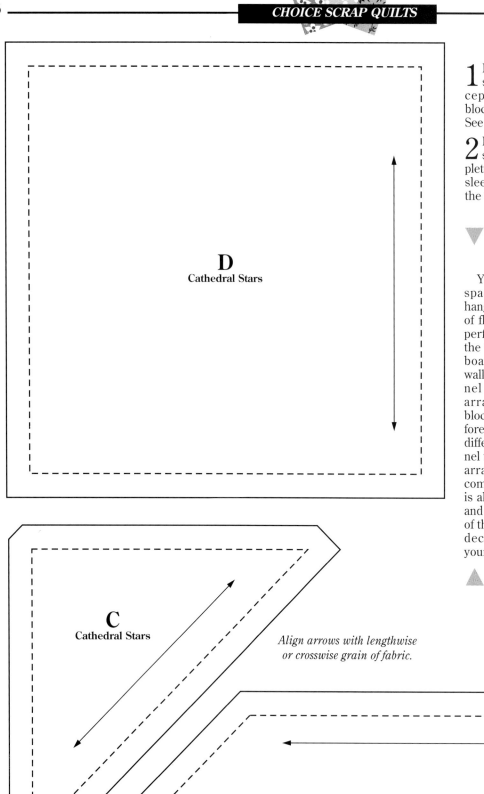

D
Cathedral Stars

C
Cathedral Stars

Align arrows with lengthwise or crosswise grain of fabric.

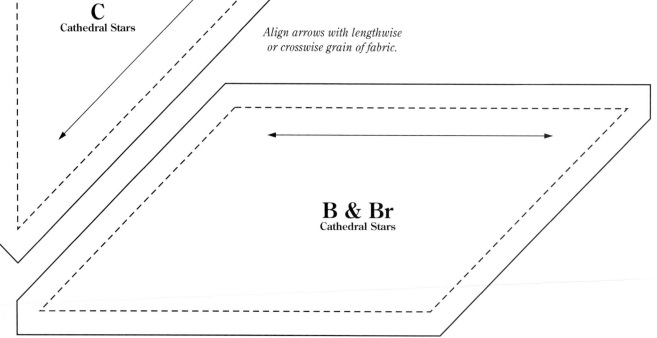

B & Br
Cathedral Stars

WALL QUILT

1 Follow the directions for the full-size version of Cathedral Stars, except make four W blocks, four X blocks, four Y blocks, and one Z block. See the wall quilt assembly diagram.

2 Follow Steps 2 through 7 in the full-size assembly instructions to complete the quilt. If desired, add a 3″-wide sleeve on the back of the quilt along the top edge for hanging with a rod.

DESIGN WALL

You can turn any wall in your sewing space into a design wall simply by hanging or mounting on it a large piece of flannel. A fuzzy flannel sheet works perfectly for this. Attach the sheet to the wall or to a freestanding foam-core board that you can prop against the wall. Fabric pressed lightly on the flannel will cling to it, allowing you to arrange and rearrange patches in blocks to determine their placement before sewing them. And you can also try different block placements on the flannel to decide on their color balance and arrangement before joining them to complete your quilt top. A design wall is also useful for trying different colors and widths of borders against an edge of the quilt top before making your final decision about which fabric frames your quilt best.

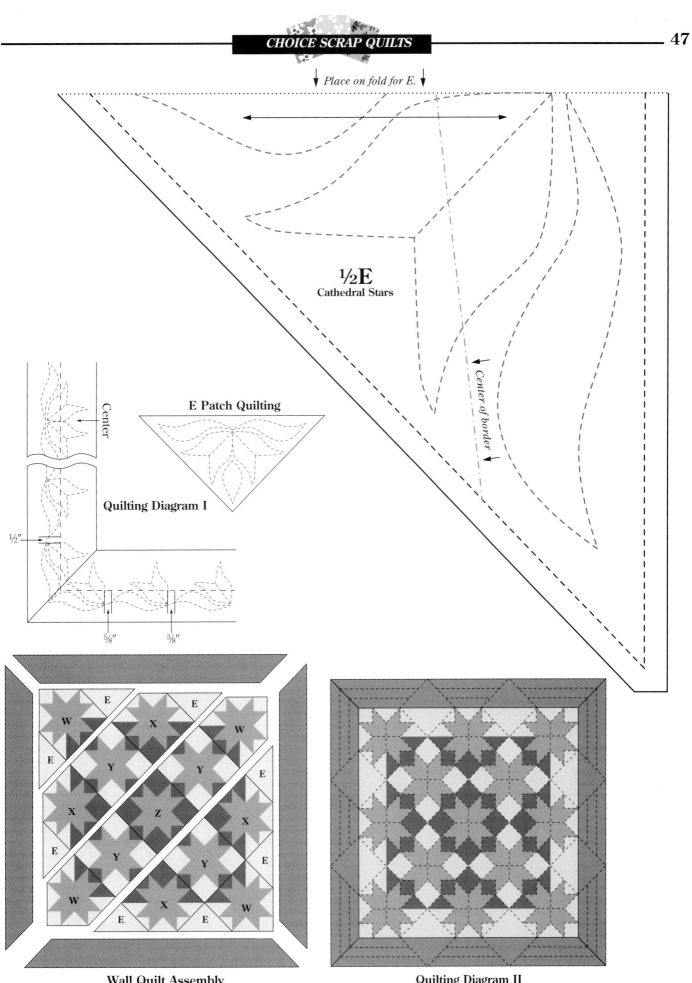

Place on fold for E.

½E
Cathedral Stars

Center of border

Center

E Patch Quilting

Quilting Diagram I

½"

5/8"   5/8"

Wall Quilt Assembly

Quilting Diagram II

Autumn Breeze

Adapted from a Susie Ennis design, made by Maria Reardon Capp and Jonna Castle

Nature provides a favorite color scheme in the autumn, and this quilt adopts it with leaves in fall's finest hues twirling as if in a gentle breeze. Capture them in a quilt to grace your bed where you can enjoy them long after the leaves outside have been raked away.

Notice how the tumbling leaves form a pinwheel in the center of each four-block section. The pinwheel effect is enhanced by the selection of two green prints for the background patches. There is a variety of colors and values within each four-block grouping. We selected gold, brown, orange, and red-rust scraps of medium-light to medium-dark values so the quilt would look balanced overall. Including very light or very dark scraps would give a spottier look that could be distracting to the overall design.

The quilt was inspired by a traditional leaf block. The block is not a difficult one to make, although care should be taken to match the diamond points in the center. Special directions in the General Instructions will help you with that. Follow them and you will find the block a breeze in more ways than one.

FULL-SIZE QUILT

Making the Blocks

1 The materials and cutting box lists the number of patches you will need to cut for this generously sized full-size quilt. Cut them from the assortment of autumn-colored scraps you have collected.

The block diagrams show how the patches go together in each of the two block colorations. Follow the diagrams carefully for correct placement of the cream and dark green D patches in the Y blocks and of the light and medium green F patches in the Z blocks. The placement of the green H patches in the Z blocks is

also important to get the pinwheel effect. Choose two autumn prints for the leaves of each block and alternate their placement.

To make it easier to get the colors correctly placed, first make one Y block,

then one Z block. Now that you have a model of each, make 23 more Y blocks and 27 more Z blocks.

Embroidering the Stems

2 Using three strands of embroidery floss in a color that coordinates with

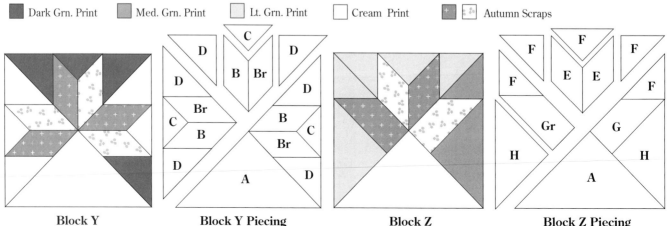

Dark Grn. Print ■ Med. Grn. Print ■ Lt. Grn. Print □ Cream Print ✛ Autumn Scraps

Block Y **Block Y Piecing** **Block Z** **Block Z Piecing**

Block Size: 10″	Full-Size Quilt	Nap/Wall Quilt
Quilt Size:	80″ x 100″	54″ x 54″
Quilt Requires:	24 Y Blocks	8 Y Blocks
	28 Z Blocks	8 Z Blocks
Materials and Cutting:		
Cream Print	**2½ yds.**	**1 yd.**
	52 A, 48 C,	16 A, 16 C,
	72 D	24 D
Lt. Grn. Print	**2⅜ yds.**	**1⅝ yds.**
2 borders	4½″ x 82½″	3½″ x 52½″
2 borders	4½″ x 62½″	3½″ x 52½″
	112 F, 28 H	32 F, 8 H
Med. Grn. Print	**¾ yd.**	**⅓ yd.**
	28 F, 28 H	8 F, 8 H
Dk. Grn. Print	**3⅛ yds.**	**1⅞ yds.**
4 borders	3½″ x 82½″	2½″ x 56½″
4 borders	3½″ x 62½″	2½″ x 46½″
binding	2½″ x 10½ yds.	2½″ x 6½ yds.
	24 C, 72 D	8 C, 24 D
Autumn Scraps	**2¼ yds.**	**1⅛ yds.**
	72 B, 72 Br,	24 B, 24 Br,
	28 E, 28 Er,	8 E, 8 Er, 8 G,
	28 G, 28 Gr	8 Gr
Lining	**7⅜ yds.**	**3½ yds.**
3 panels	35¼″ x 84″	
2 panels		29½″ x 58″
Batting	**84″ x 104″**	**58″ x 58″**

Supplies: Embroidery floss to coordinate with the scrap fabrics.

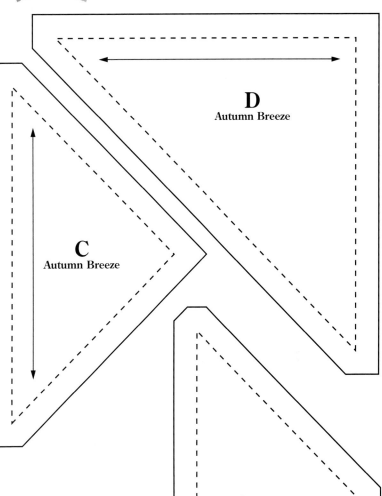

C
Autumn Breeze

D
Autumn Breeze

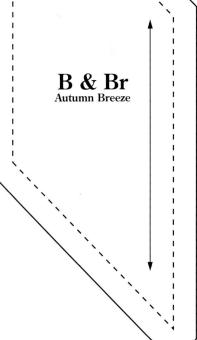

B & Br
Autumn Breeze

the scraps in each block, embroider the stems. We suggest using the chain stitch for this purpose, because it is an easy stitch that gives the weight and texture needed. The chain stitch is illustrated on the next page.

Arranging the Blocks
3 First, set aside four Z blocks for use in the corners of the borders. Now you are ready to arrange your blocks to form the four-block units. To begin, look at the photograph of the quilt. Notice that each four-block unit is made with either four Y blocks or four Z blocks, each rotated once clockwise beginning from the top left of the block. You will want to arrange blocks on a table top until you get the color balance you like.

Pin them together in the order you have planned. Do this with several groups of four blocks to make sure the color arrangement in the units is working out to your satisfaction. Arrange and pin all the blocks into a total of 12 four-block units.

Refer to the quilt photo again. Arrange the four-block units so that the Y-block units alternate with the Z-block units in each row. Play with the arrangement until

the balance of colors and contrasts pleases you. Repin the arrangement of some of the blocks in the units if necessary.

Assembling the Quilt Top
4 Now stitch each unit together. After they are completed, press them as explained in the General Instructions. Join the units into four rows of three each, and press each row. Join the four rows and press again.

5 Matching their centers, sew a short dark green border to each side of a light green border. Repeat. In the same manner, sew the long dark and light green borders together.

Sew a Z block to each end of the short border units, rotating the blocks as indicated in the quilt photograph. Sew the long borders to the sides of the quilt top. Press, then sew the short borders to the top and bottom.

Taking It to the Finish
6 Mark the top with quilting motifs we've provided, or as you desire. Sew the lining panels together. Layer the lining, batting, and top as explained in the General Instructions. Pin or baste the layers together.

7 We suggest in-the-ditch quilting around the leaves to define them. We added stipple machine quilting in the large plain A patches. A figure showing the stipple quilting is shown on the following page. The stippling flattens those areas somewhat, making the leaves stand out in relief. We also stipple quilted in the border. Quilt the patches as marked or as you desire.

8 Finally, finish the edges of the quilt with double-fold binding as explained in the General Instructions. Don't forget to sign and date your quilt on the back!

NAP/WALL QUILT

This smaller quilt is designed with narrower border strips that are mitered rather than set with the corner blocks.

1 Piece and embroider eight Y and eight Z blocks as instructed in Steps 1 and 2 of the full-size quilt assembly.

2 Join four Y blocks or four Z blocks to make a four-block unit, rotating the blocks as shown in the diagram. Join four four-block units, alternating them as shown.

3 Matching centers, sew a dark green border to each side of a light green border. Repeat for a total of 4 border units. Sew borders to the the quilt, beginning and ending stitches ¼" from the edges of the quilt. Miter the corners, trimming excess border fabric to leave ¼" seam allowances.

4 Follow Steps 6 through 8 from full-size assembly to complete the quilt. If desired, add a 3"-wide sleeve on the back of the quilt along the top edge for hanging with a rod.

Nap/Wall Quilt Assembly

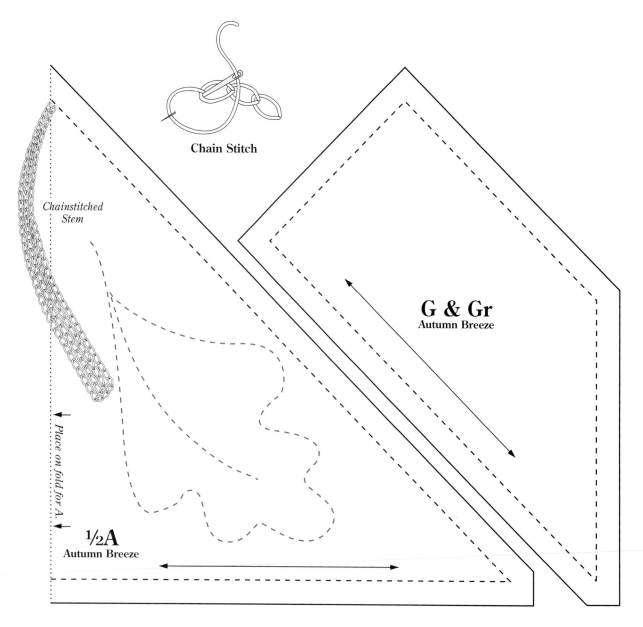

Chain Stitch

Chainstitched Stem

Place on fold for A.

½A
Autumn Breeze

G & Gr
Autumn Breeze

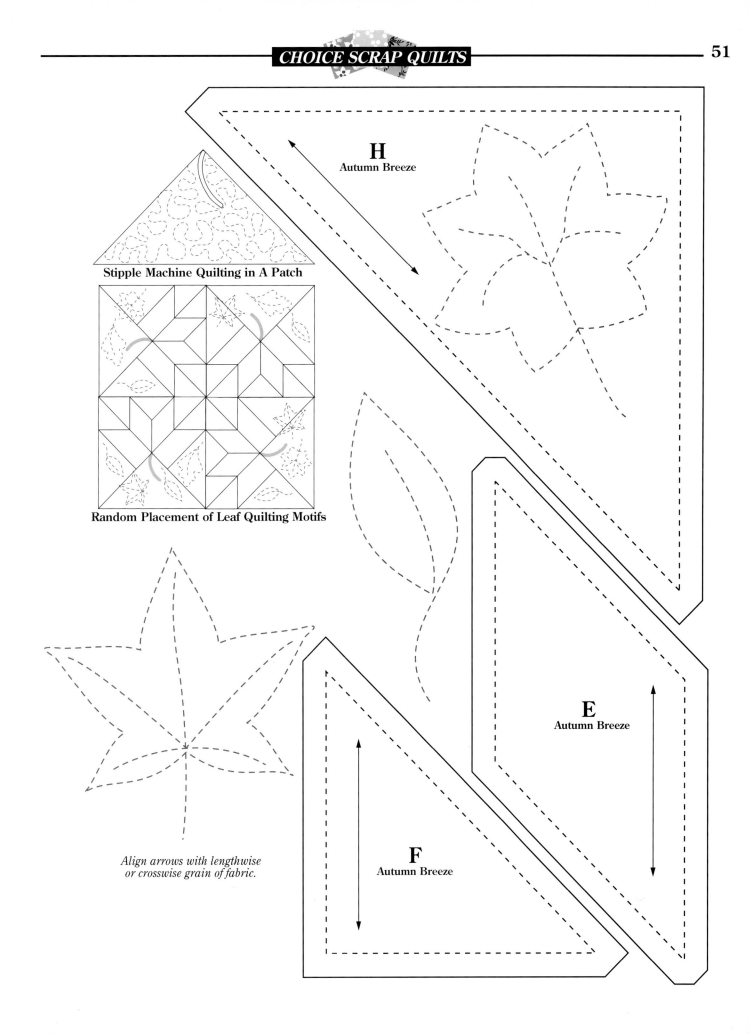

H
Autumn Breeze

Stipple Machine Quilting in A Patch

Random Placement of Leaf Quilting Motifs

E
Autumn Breeze

F
Autumn Breeze

*Align arrows with lengthwise
or crosswise grain of fabric.*

Color Twists

Adapted from a Nancy Cabot design, made by Nancy Fisher and Terri Belke

This quilt is a modern color variation of an old block called Triple Link Chain. The block's construction offers a delightful way to use scraps from all the color families you have in your fabric collection. In each block, the eight B patches cut from medium-bright shades in a color family form a vibrant twisting circle around the paler octagonal patch in the center. Surrounding each "twist" with the textured look of a white-on-white print frames it with sparkle. Using two light green scraps in opposing block corners and two dark green scraps in the remaining corners adds a secondary design when the blocks are joined. Selecting a single dark green fabric for the border and diamond shapes gives unity to the design and holds the scrappy elements together. If you choose a stripe, you will want to place the D and Dr patches on the stripe so that when they are sewn together at the block edges, the stripes will match. The patterned chevrons that result add another twist to the overall design.

FULL-SIZE QUILT

Cutting and Sewing the Blocks

1 To achieve the look of the quilt in the photograph, for each block cut eight medium scrap B's and one light

scrap A. Cut other patches as specified in the materials and cutting box. Note the placement of D and Dr patches on the stripe as shown on the opposite page. Keep patches color sorted throughout the piecing.

2 When piecing each block, sew the first B patch to an A patch in a partial seam as follows: Sew a B patch to the A patch, sewing only halfway down the edge of A. Open flat and finger press B. (See figures below.)

Working counter-clockwise, sew remaining B's to the A in complete seams. Finish the partial seam of the

Block

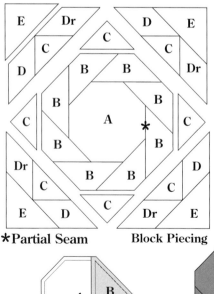

*Partial Seam   Block Piecing

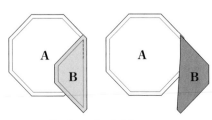

Sewing a Partial Seam

Adding the Next B Patch

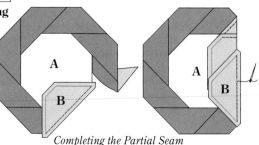

Completing the Partial Seam

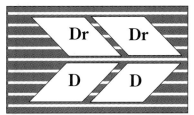

D and Dr Patches on Striped Fabric

first B patch. Press seam allowances away from the A patch.

Look at the block piecing diagram and complete the block by sewing the remaining patches to the A/B unit. If you use a stripe for the D and Dr patches, you will want to be careful to place them so that the stripe runs the length of the patch as shown in the block diagram. Make 42 blocks. Press.

Assembling the Quilt Top

3 Use a large, flat surface to arrange the blocks in seven rows of six blocks each until a pleasing order is found. Rotate the blocks so that the dark green E's are in the top left and bottom right corners. Join blocks in rows. Press rows and join them, carefully matching the points of white C patches and green E patches where they meet. Press again.

4 Fold a short border in half to find the center. Then, fold the quilt top in half both directions to find the centers of each side. Matching their centers, pin and sew a short border to top edge. Repeat at the bottom. Matching centers again, sew the long borders to the sides, mitering the corners. Instructions for mitering corners are found in the General Instructions. Trim the excess to leave ¼″ seam allowances.

Taking It to the Finish

5 Mark the floral quilting motif in the A patches. If you want to use the border quilting motif, place its center in the middle of one border, then move it along, repeatedly placing it end to end and marking it until you get to the seam of the corner miter. Depending on the size of the quilt you are making, the motifs will meet at the miters in a slightly different design. Simply shorten or lengthen the stems, and add or subtract a leaf until you are pleased with the design. Remember to begin the motif in the middle of each border and work toward the sides for the best results.

If you choose a stripe for your borders, you may prefer to omit the motif and follow one or more of the stripes with quilting.

6 Sew the lining panels together. Layer quilt lining, batting, and top as explained in the General Instructions; pin or thread-baste the layers together.

7 Quilt motifs as marked. Quilt in-the-ditch around the patches, and quilt the border with the border motif provided. Apply double-fold binding to finish the quilt, as described in the General Instructions.

QUEEN-SIZE QUILT

1 Piece 56 blocks as described in Steps 1 and 2 of the full-size assembly instructions. Arrange and sew the blocks in eight rows of seven blocks each and join the rows.

2 Follow the remaining steps of the full-size assembly to complete the queen-size quilt.

Block Size: 12″	Full-Size Quilt 78″ x 90″	Queen-Size Quilt 90″ x 102″
Materials and Cutting:		
White Print	1¾ yds. 336 C	2¼ yds. 448 C
Lt. Scraps	1⅛ yds. 42 A	1½ yds. 56 A
Med. Scraps	2⅞ yds. 336 B	3⅞ yds. 448 B
Lt. Grn. Scraps	⅞ yd. 84 E	1⅛ yds. 112 E
Dk. Grn. Scraps	⅞ yd. 84 E	1⅛ yds. 112 E
Green Stripe 2 borders 2 borders binding	3¾ yds. 3½″ x 92½″ 3½″ x 80½″ 2½″ x 10¼ yds. 168 D, 168 Dr	4⅝ yds. 3½″ x 104½″ 3½″ x 92½″ 2½″ x 11⅝ yds. 224 D, 224 Dr
Lining 3 panels	7¼ yds. 31⅞″ x 82″	8¼ yds. 35⅞″ x 94″
Batting	82″ x 94″	94″ x 106″

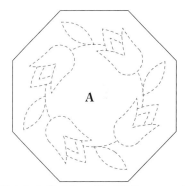

Patch A Quilting Motif Placement

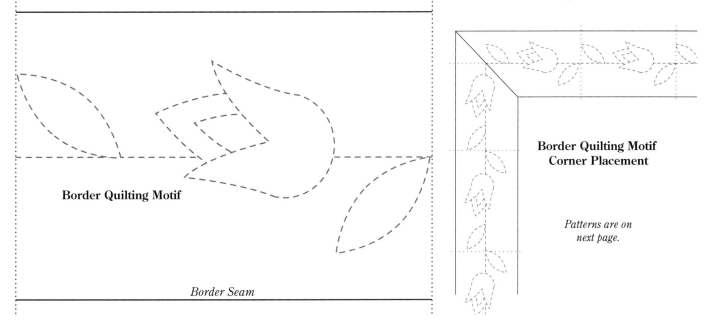

Border Quilting Motif

Border Seam

Border Quilting Motif Corner Placement

Patterns are on next page.

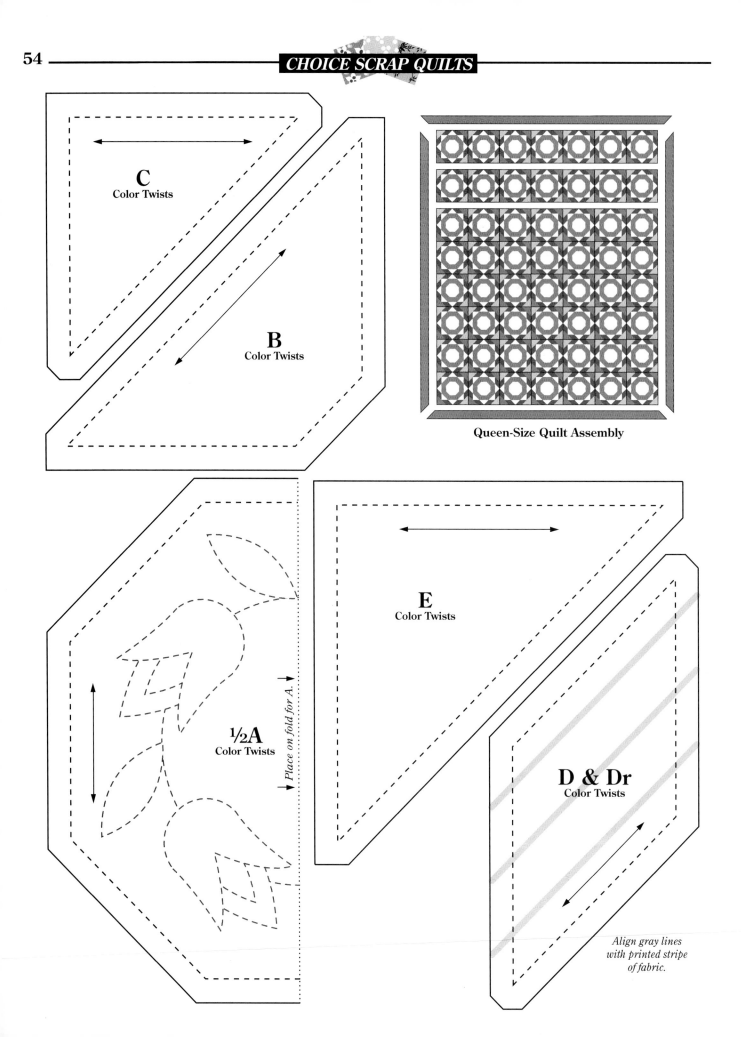

C
Color Twists

B
Color Twists

Queen-Size Quilt Assembly

E
Color Twists

½A
Color Twists

Place on fold for A.

D & Dr
Color Twists

*Align gray lines
with printed stripe
of fabric.*

Calico Mosaic

Adapted from a Nancy Cabot design, made by Carolee Miller and Carla Kilkelly

Cheerful print fabrics in every hue dance across this easy quilt that will sparkle on your bed or wall. Reminiscent of a beautifully elaborate tile design, the corners of each block are colored to bring out an effect of diamond-like squares that float at each block corner and into the easy-to-piece border. The center of each block is a mix of light and dark colors, surrounded in block Y by multicolored dark scraps and in block Z by multicolored light scraps. We've tied this quilt with an invisible tying method described in the General Instructions, but quilting directions are included in the assembly instructions.

FULL-SIZE QUILT

Planning and Sewing the Blocks

1 Sort your scraps into light prints, yellow prints, dark prints, and dark solids. Cut out the necessary number of patches as listed in the materials and cutting box. Find a flat area where you can arrange patches for one Y block and one Z block. Keep referring to the block Y and block Z drawings to keep track of light/dark color placement so that you can maintain the alternating light and dark outer rings around the blocks. Experiment with color placement until you find combinations that you like. Then, make 13 Y blocks and 12 Z blocks.

Assembling the Quilt Top

2 Look at the color photo of the quilt. This quilt has a very easy set, with blocks set directly against each other. For the first row, alternately join three block Y's (dark outer patches) and two block Z's (light outer patches) to make

a row, starting the row with a block Y. Repeat to make three rows like this and set the three rows aside, to be joined later with alternating color rows. Start a new row with a block Z and alternately join three block Z's and two block Y's. Repeat to make two rows like this. Join rows, with odd-numbered rows beginning with a block Y and even-numbered rows beginning with a block Z.

Adding the Borders

3 The pieced border is really very easy. Just pay attention to the bor-

der unit diagrams to get the floating-diamonds effect. Gather your F patches and the rest of the light green print C's and dark solid C's. Look at the border unit diagrams and join patches to make 12 border unit 1's, eight border unit 2's, and four border unit 3's. Alternately join three unit 1's and two unit 2's to complete one border. Make three more borders like the one you just completed. Fold each border in half to find the center of the strip. Then, fold the quilt top in half both

■ Dark Solid Scraps	▨ Dark Print Scraps	□ Muslin
▨ Yellow Scraps	▨ Light Green Print	▨ Light Print Scraps

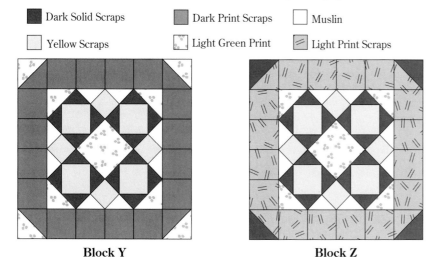

Block Y   **Block Z**

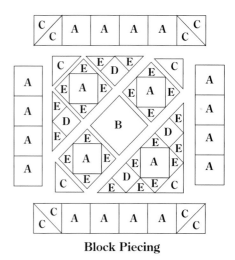

Block Piecing

Block Size:	Full-Size	Wall
15″	Quilt	Quilt
Quilt Size:	80″ x 80″	50″ x 50″
Quilt Requires:	13 Y Blocks	5 Y Blocks
	12 Z Blocks	4 Z Blocks

Materials and Cutting:

Dk. Print Scraps	2 yds.	⅞ yd.
	208 A, 52 C	80 A, 20 C
Dk. Solid Scraps	1¾ yds.	¾ yd.
	72 C, 400 E	32 C, 144 E
Lt. Print Scraps	1¾ yds.	¾ yd.
	192 A, 48 C	64 A, 16 C
Yellow Scraps	1¼ yds.	⅝ yd.
	100 A, 100 D	36 A, 36 D
Lt. Green Print	1¼ yds.	⅝ yd.
	25 B, 176 C	9 B, 68 C
Muslin	¾ yd.	⅜ yd.
	200 E	72 E
Med. Blue Print	1 yd.	⅝ yd.
	4 C, 20 F	4 C, 12 F
Binding	⅞ yd.	⅝ yd.
	2½″ x 9¾ yds.	2½″ x 6⅛ yds.
Lining	7⅜ yds.	3¼ yds.
3 panels	28½″ x 84″	
2 panels		27½″ x 54″
Batting	84″ x 84″	54″ x 54″

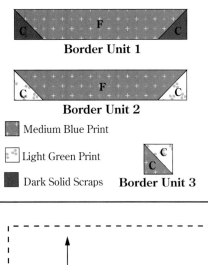

Border Unit 1

Border Unit 2

■ Medium Blue Print

▫ Light Green Print

■ Dark Solid Scraps **Border Unit 3**

ways to find the center of each side. Sew two of the borders you made to the two side edges of the quilt top, matching centers and placing the shorter sides of the F patches next to the quilt blocks. Add a unit 3 to each end of the remaining borders, being careful to turn the corner units so that the color placement is correct. Keep referring to the quilt photo as necessary. Sew these borders to the top and bottom of the quilt top, again matching centers and placing the shorter sides of the F patches next to the quilt blocks.

Taking It to the Finish

4 Sew the lining panels together. Press the quilt top and the lining, then mark our special quilting motif in the B and F patches if you are quilting instead of tying. Assemble and baste the lining, batting, and quilt top as explained in the General Instructions.

5 If you prefer to tie your quilt, we suggest that you place the ties in the blocks as shown in the tying grid diagram on this page. If you plan to quilt, we suggest outline quilting all but the B and F patches ¼″ from seams. This will emphasize the mosaic quality of the design. Quilt the B's and F's as marked. When you have finished your quilting, apply double-fold binding to finish, as described in the General Instructions. Remember to sign and date your quilt on the back, either with permanent pen or embroidery, and you might want to use a special label too.

WALL QUILT

1 Follow the instructions given in Step 1 of the full-size assembly, but make only five Y blocks and four Z blocks.

2 Look at the wall quilt assembly diagram. You will see that you need to alternately join two dark Y blocks and one light Z block to make the top and bottom rows. For the middle row, alternately join two light blocks and one dark block. Join rows.

3 Follow the instructions in Step 3 of the full-size assembly, except that for the wall quilt you only need to make eight border unit 1's, four border unit 2's, and four border unit 3's. Sew one border unit 2 between two border unit 1's to make a border. Repeat to make four borders like this. Sew two of the borders to the sides of the quilt top, matching centers and placing the shorter sides of the F patches next to the quilt blocks. For the two remaining borders, add a border unit 3 to each end. Then sew those two borders to the top and bottom of the quilt top, matching centers and placing the shorter sides of the F patches next to quilt blocks.

4 Sew the lining panels together. Press the top and lining, then mark the quilting motif in the B and F patches if you are quilting instead of tying. Assemble and baste the lining, batting, and quilt top.

5 Tie your quilt, or quilt B's and F's as marked and outline quilt the remaining patches ¼″ from seams. Apply double-fold binding to finish. If desired, add a 3″-wide sleeve on the back of the quilt along the top edge to hang with a rod.

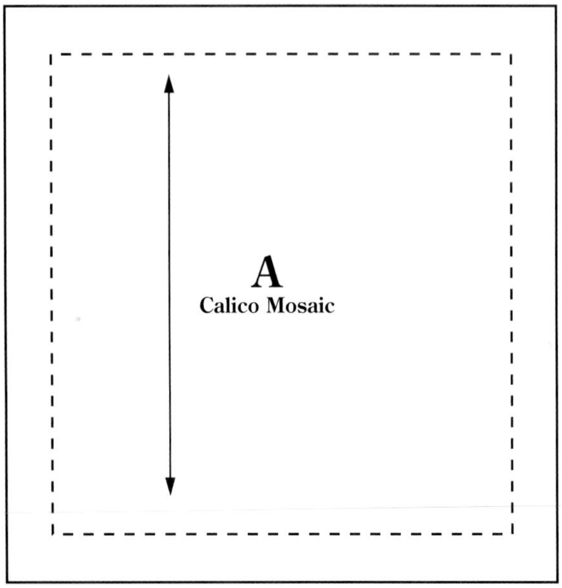

A
Calico Mosaic

D
Calico Mosaic

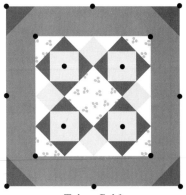

Tying Grid

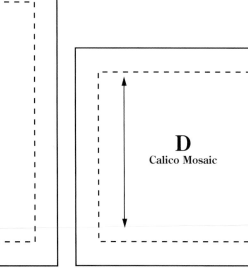

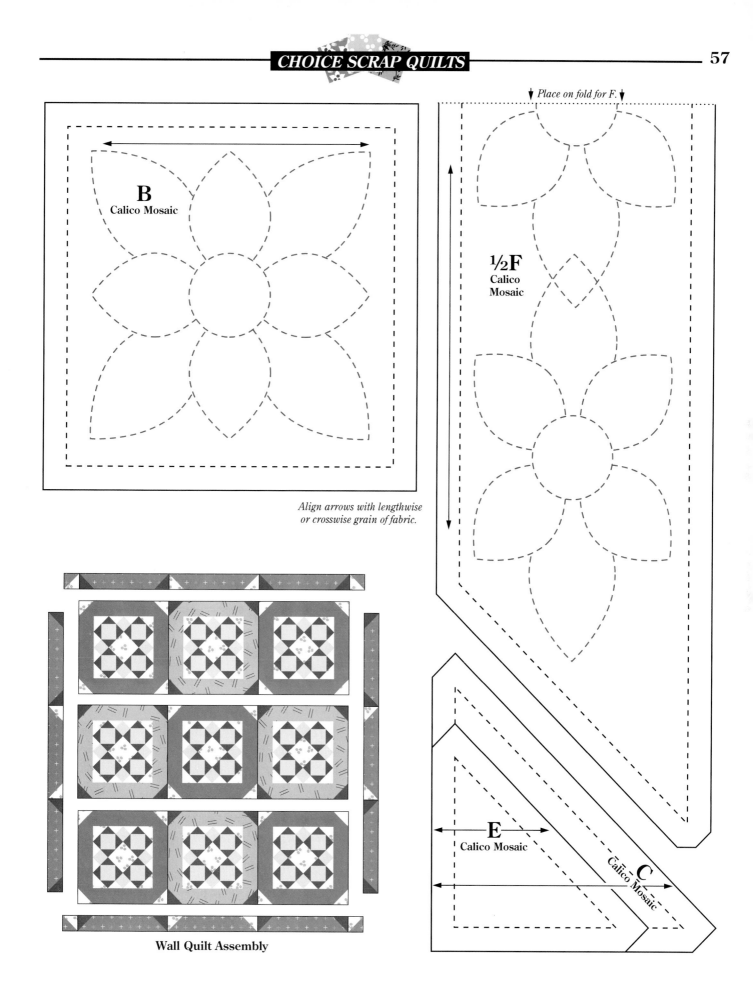

B
Calico Mosaic

*Align arrows with lengthwise
or crosswise grain of fabric.*

Place on fold for F.

½F
Calico
Mosaic

E
Calico Mosaic

C
Calico Mosaic

Wall Quilt Assembly

Second Time Around

Designed by Theresa Eisinger, made by Libby Phillips

    This pattern is ideal for a planned scrap quilt. That term usually refers to a structured design in which various colors of scraps are placed in an organized, repeat arrangement. But a planned scrap quilt can also be the happy outcome when you buy a big piece of a beautiful print you love, but you don't quite know what to do with it. Don't put it on the shelf and wait for inspiration. Instead, select three of the prettiest colors from it. Go to your fabric stash and find all your scraps in those three color families. To tie everything together, choose one more blending print in a shade of the starting print's predominant color. Use this fabric as an outer border frame and for a few of the patches in the blocks.

    Look at the color photograph of Second Time Around on page 32, and you will see how that plan worked for us. We started with a green background print covered with flowers and leaves. From its posies we picked up the red/pink, yellow/gold, and green families. We chose a dark green tone-on-tone print for its outer border. The resulting quilt is delightfully exuberant.

    The square in the center of each block is big enough to show off a special commemorative print or an interesting conversation print. This pattern also offers an opportunity to use one of the contemporary art prints that you love but find difficult to combine with other fabrics. Your collection of scraps is the answer.

TWIN-SIZE QUILT

Making the Blocks

1 Prepare templates and mark fabric as explained in the General Instructions. Cut out the borders and the A squares first. Then from the remaining yardage and your scraps, cut the number of patches listed in the box.

2 Guided by the block piecing diagram, stitch a C triangle between two B diamonds. Make four of these B/C/B units. Attach one of them to each side of an A square and join them at the corners.

3 Stitch a C triangle between D and Dr patches. Make four of these units. Stitch one to opposite sides of the block. Attach an E square to each end of the remaining two units, and sew them to the top and bottom to complete the block. Make a total of 24 blocks.

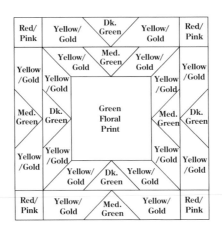

Block Piecing

Block Size:	Twin-Size
15¾″	**Quilt**
Quilt Size:	74¾″ x 106¼″

Materials and Cutting:

Green Floral Print	3 yds.
2 borders	2⅞″ x 101¾″
2 borders	2⅞″ x 70¼″
	24 A
Dk. Green Print	**3¼ yds.**
2 borders	4″ x 108¾″
2 borders	4″ x 77¼″
binding	2½″ x 11 yds.
Yellow/Gold Scraps	**3⅞ yds.**
	192 B, 96 D,
	96 Dr
Med. Green Scraps	**⅞ yd.**
	96 C
Dk. Green Scraps	**⅞ yd.**
	96 C
Red/Pink Scraps	**¾ yd.**
	96 E
Lining	**6½ yds.**
2 panels	40″ x 110¼″
Batting	**78¾″ x 110¼″**

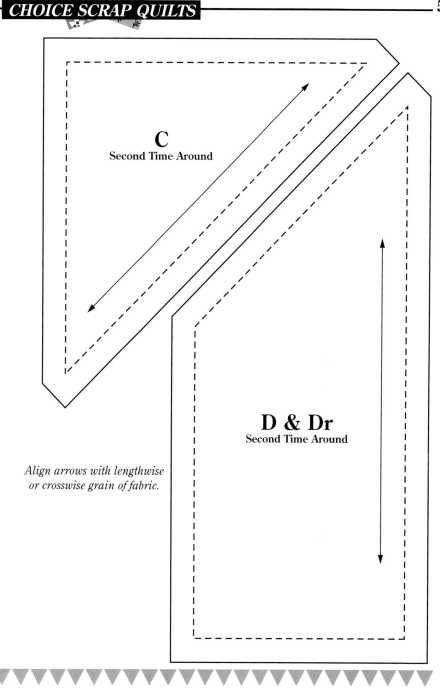

C
Second Time Around

D & Dr
Second Time Around

Align arrows with lengthwise or crosswise grain of fabric.

Assembling the Top

4 Join blocks in six rows of four blocks each, turning the blocks so that the medium and dark green patches are in the correct position. Press.

5 Sew the inner and outer border strips together in pairs, two long pairs and two short pairs. Press and fold each border in half crosswise to mark its center. Sew the short borders to the top and bottom, matching their centers. Sew the two long borders to the sides. Miter the corners, referring to the General Instructions.

Taking It to the Finish

6 Mark the quilting pattern given, or the pattern of your choice, in each A patch. Refer to the border quilting diagram to mark motifs with five complete petals. Center a motif on each mitered corner, then space motifs along the borders, noting that the petals cross the seam between the two border strips.

Sew the lining panels together. Layer the lining, batting, and top; baste. Outline quilting or in-the-ditch quilting is suggested for the remaining patches. When you complete your quilting, apply double-fold binding and remember to sign and date your quilt.

QUILT SIZE VARIATIONS

The size in which this quilt is made works as a spread for a twin bed and as a coverlet for a double bed. This pattern can be adjusted easily to make several other quilt sizes also.

When changing the size of this quilt, or any quilt in this book, the amount of yardage for borders and binding may need to be adjusted.

Double- or Queen-Size, 90½″ x 106¼″. Sew six more blocks and add one to the end of each row before assembling the rows. The blocks will be set in six rows of five each. Increase the length of top and bottom border strips to 86″. No additional yardage of the two border prints will be required.

King-Size, 106¼″ x 106¼″. Add two rows of blocks to the width of the quilt to make it square. Set the 36 blocks six by six. You will need about 1½ times as many scraps in each color family. The yardage for the borders given for the twin-size quilt is sufficient.

Wall Quilt, 43¼″ x 43¼″. Join four blocks to make a square, add borders. Only 1⅜ yards of each border fabric will be required.

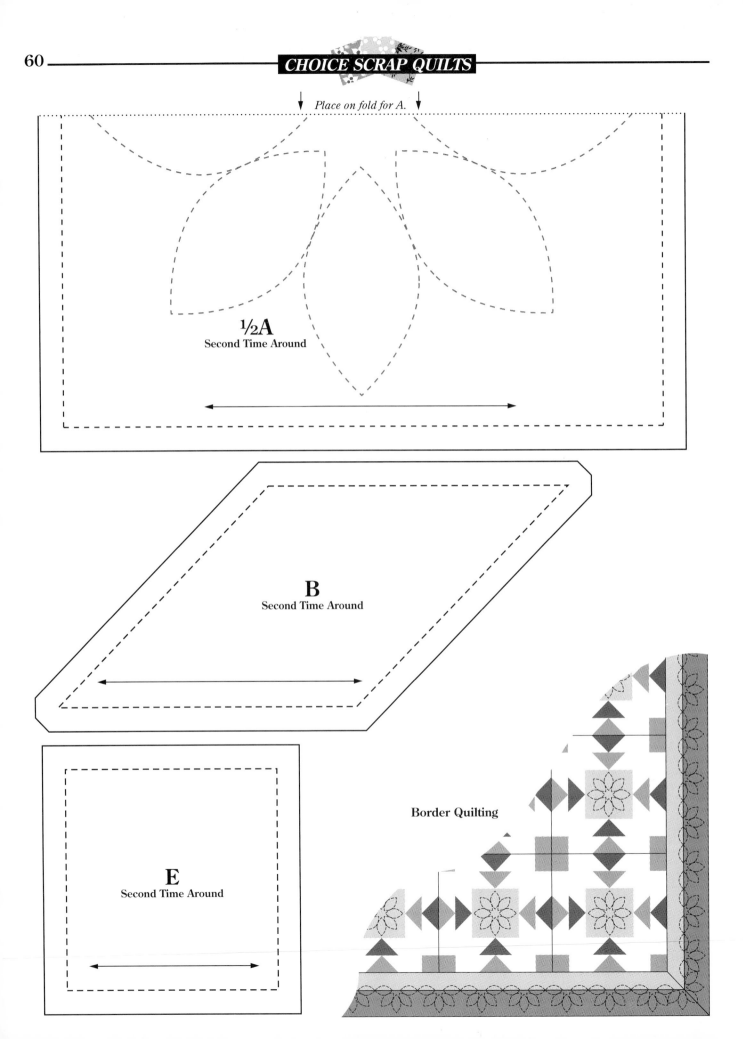

Place on fold for A.

½A
Second Time Around

B
Second Time Around

E
Second Time Around

Border Quilting

Hearts and Flowers

Designed by Dorothy Fischer, made by Nancy Fisher

Here is a quilt to express your love for someone special. It combines easy-to-piece hearts made of simple squares and half-square triangles. You can use your darker or brighter scraps for them. The patches surrounding the hearts can be in light shades of a neutral color to tie all the blocks together. We used pastel solids for the sashing as a nice contrast to the patterned fabrics and brighter solids for the easy-to-appliqué flowers and leaves in the sashing. This is a good pattern for emptying out your scrapbag, whether you make a bed quilt or wall quilt.

TWIN-SIZE QUILT

Making the Blocks

1 Before you begin to make the blocks, you may want to sort your scraps by color. The materials and cutting box tells you how many patches to cut from each color. You will need 20 A and 10 B bright print patches for each heart shape plus 6 A and 10 B patches for the cream background of each block. Referring to the block piecing diagram, piece the A's and B's in rows, then join the rows. Add a C to each side, then a D to the top and the bottom to complete one block.

You can take advantage of chain piecing, described on page 69, to assemble the 20 blocks needed for the twin-size quilt.

Sashes and Setting Squares

2 To make a sash, join eight pastel A's to form a row. Then make a second row and join the two rows lengthwise to complete the sash. The twin size requires 49 sashes. To form a setting square, join four pastel A's in two rows of two. There is a total of 30 setting squares.

Assembling the Quilt Top

3 If you prefer to appliqué the flowers and leaves to the sashes and setting squares before assembling the top, refer to Step 4 and do so now.

Lay out all the blocks and sashes on a large, flat surface and try various ways of assembling the quilt to find the color arrangement you like best.

Sew five sashes alternately with four blocks to form a block row. You will need five block rows. Then join five setting squares alternately with four sashes to form a sash row. Make six sash

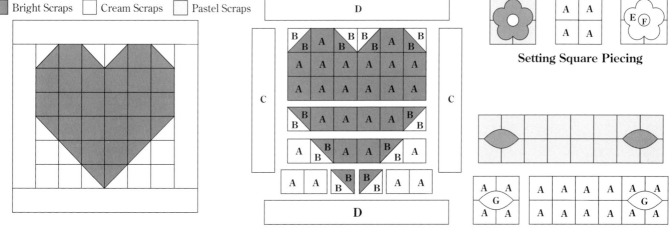

Bright Scraps □ Cream Scraps □ Pastel Scraps

Block Piecing

Setting Square Piecing

Sash Piecing

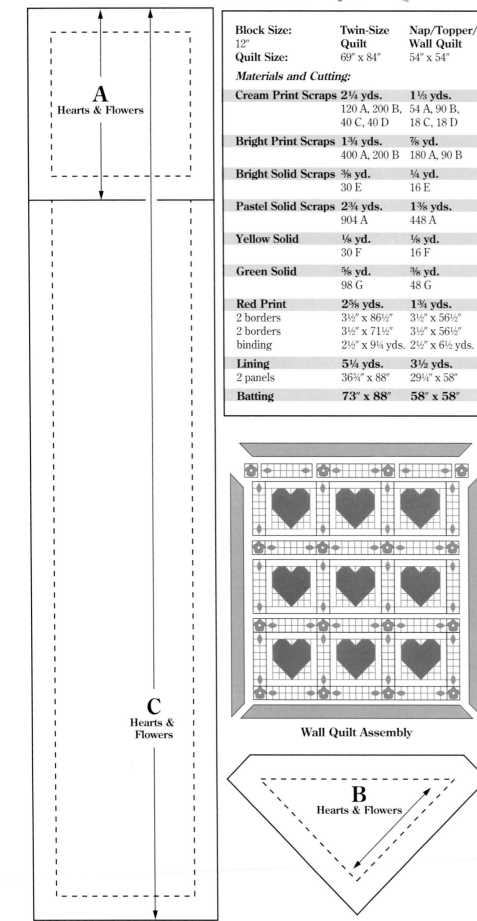

Block Size: 12"	Twin-Size Quilt	Nap/Topper/ Wall Quilt
Quilt Size:	69" x 84"	54" x 54"
Materials and Cutting:		
Cream Print Scraps	2¼ yds.	1⅓ yds.
	120 A, 200 B, 40 C, 40 D	54 A, 90 B, 18 C, 18 D
Bright Print Scraps	1¾ yds.	⅞ yd.
	400 A, 200 B	180 A, 90 B
Bright Solid Scraps	⅜ yd.	¼ yd.
	30 E	16 E
Pastel Solid Scraps	2¾ yds.	1⅜ yds.
	904 A	448 A
Yellow Solid	⅛ yd.	⅛ yd.
	30 F	16 F
Green Solid	⅝ yd.	⅜ yd.
	98 G	48 G
Red Print	2⅝ yds.	1¾ yds.
2 borders	3½" x 86½"	3½" x 56½"
2 borders	3½" x 71½"	3½" x 56½"
binding	2½" x 9¼ yds.	2½" x 6½ yds.
Lining	5¼ yds.	3½ yds.
2 panels	36¾" x 88"	29¼" x 58"
Batting	73" x 88"	58" x 58"

Wall Quilt Assembly

rows. Starting with a sash row, join all the rows, alternating sash rows and block rows.

Appliquéing the Patches

4 To prepare the appliqués for sewing, turn under ³⁄₁₆" allowances on all patches and baste the allowances in place. Place the flowers and leaves on the setting squares and sashes as shown in the photo, and pin them in place. You can sew the appliqués on by hand or machine.

Attaching the Borders

5 To miter the corners, matching centers, sew a long border to each side of the quilt. Again matching centers, sew a short border to the top of the quilt and repeat for the bottom. Miter the corners as described in the General Instructions. Trim the corners to leave ¼" seam allowances.

Taking It to the Finish

6 Decide on your quilting plan. This quilt would be pretty tied, if you prefer. As a quilting suggestion, you can quilt in-the-ditch around each heart. Then stitch two or three progressively smaller concentric heart shapes within the pieced heart, as shown in the block quilting diagram. A quilting motif with double hearts and a ribbon is given to fit in the border. Mark one heart in each border corner, then add the motifs, spacing them to fill the border.

7 Sew the lining panels together. Layer the lining, batting, and quilt top. Baste the quilt "sandwich," using either needle and thread or safety pins. Quilt the motifs you have marked. Quilt in-the-ditch around patches in the sashes and setting squares. Apply double-fold binding as described in the General Instructions to finish the quilt edges.

WALL QUILT

1 Follow Step 1 in the twin-size assembly directions, except that you will need to make only nine blocks.

2 Sashes for the wall quilt are made the same way as in Step 2 for the twin size. The wall quilt needs only 24 sashes and 16 setting squares.

3 Join four sashes alternately with three blocks to form a block row. Make three block rows. Then join four setting squares alternately with three sashes to form a sash row. Make four sash rows. Sew the rows together, alternating types.

4 Use Steps 4 through 7 in the twin-size instructions to finish the wall quilt. You can add a 3"-wide sleeve on the back top edge to make it easier to hang.

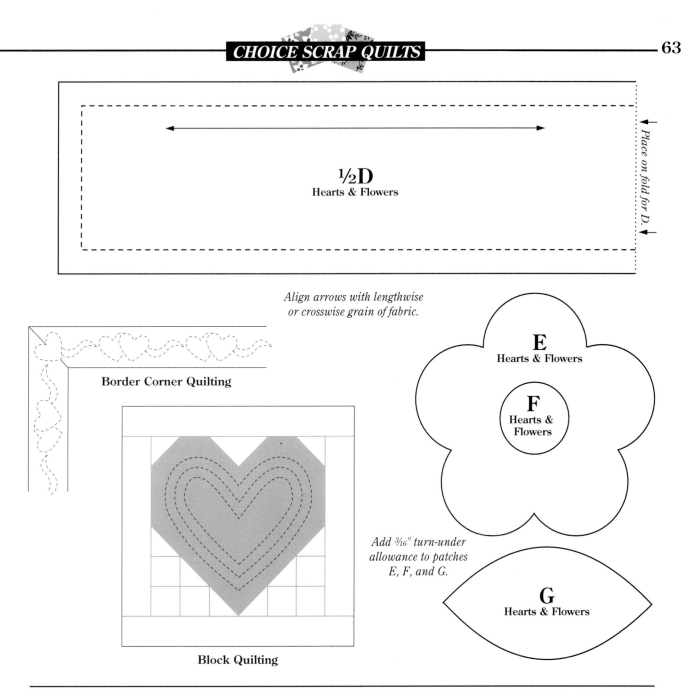

½D
Hearts & Flowers

Place on fold for D.

*Align arrows with lengthwise
or crosswise grain of fabric.*

Border Corner Quilting

E
Hearts & Flowers

F
Hearts &
Flowers

Block Quilting

*Add ³⁄₁₆″ turn-under
allowance to patches
E, F, and G.*

G
Hearts & Flowers

Border Seam

Border Seam

Border Quilting Motif

Blues in the Night

Designed by Karen Gillis Taylor, made by Maria Reardon Capp and Peggy Spradlin

If blue and teal are among your favorite colors, you probably have a wonderful accumulation of scraps in those hues waiting to be used in this simple-to-make pattern. (Be sure to check the color pages for another color combination if blues aren't up your alley.) Why not try a wall quilt of this pattern in a different color family? Keep the light, medium, and dark scraps in the same position as in Blues in the Night to get the same overall pattern.

FULL-SIZE QUILT

Planning and Sewing the Blocks

1 Sort your scraps into light, medium, and dark blue/teal scraps. Cut the number of patches listed. Remember to cut the borders from your border fabrics before you cut the patches.

Look carefully at the block diagram to become familiar with where the colors are placed. All of the pattern pieces are cut from more than one fabric, so you will need to pay attention to where they are placed.

2 This block is easily constructed in diagonal rows, as you can see in the block piecing diagram. Lay out all of the patches for one block before you begin, and be sure to stitch the correct edges of the patches together to form the design. Also, if you handle the bias edges carefully, you won't stretch them out of shape while you make the block. When you pin the rows to stitch them together, the seams will cross ¼″ in from the edge. If you stitch exactly through that point, the seams will meet accurately. Make one block to be sure you have the color placement correct, then use that block as a guide when making the other 47 blocks.

Assembling the Quilt Top

3 If you look at the quilt photo, you will see that four blocks are rotated to form a larger block. Stitch 12 of these larger units. Stitch three together to form a row. Make four rows. Stitch the four rows together.

4 Fold all of the border pieces in half to find the center of the long edges and mark with a crease. Matching centers, sew one short white/blue border to one short bright blue print border along the long edge. Sew one short navy border to the bright blue print border to make a three-border unit. Repeat for the remaining short borders. Sew

one three-border unit to the top of the quilt, matching the center of the borders to the center of the quilt top. Begin and end stitching ¼″ from the edge of the quilt. (The extra fabric on the ends is used to miter the corners.)

Sew the other three-border unit to the bottom of the quilt. Repeat this procedure for the long borders and sew them to the sides of the quilt. Miter the corners by following the directions for multiple mitered borders in the Gener-

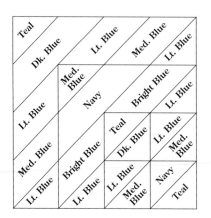

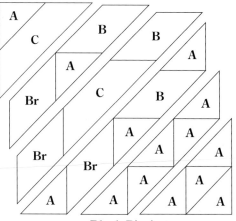

Block Piecing

᠁nstructions. Press the quilt top.

᠁ the lining panels together.
᠁he seam allowances open.

the Finish

᠁uilt lining, batting, and
᠁hread-baste the layers

᠁ quilt with an invis-
᠁d described in the
᠁. A tying grid for
᠁on this page. If
᠁a suggestion.
᠁f patches.
᠁᠁m out-
᠁᠁᠁bor-
᠁᠁᠁᠁᠁e

᠁r
᠁y ᠁

WALL QUILT

1 Sort your fabrics as described in Step 1 of the full-size quilt instructions. The materials and cutting box tells you how many of each patch to cut from each of the fabrics.

2 Make 16 blocks as described in Step 2 of the full-size quilt instructions.

3 Rotate and stitch the blocks together in four units of four as shown in the wall quilt diagram. Make two rows of two blocks each. Stitch the rows together and press the top.

4 Sew the lining panels together. Layer quilt lining, batting, and quilt top; baste. Tie or quilt and bind to finish as described in Step 7 above. If desired, ᠁dd a 3"-wide sleeve on the back of the ᠁'t along the top edge for hanging with ᠁(see the General Instructions).

Tying Grid

Block size: 10"		
Quilt size:		x 53"

Materials and C᠁		
Lt. Blue Scraps		⅞ yd.
		96 A, 16 B, 16 Br
Med. Blue Scrap᠁	᠁ ds.	⅝ yd.
	144 A, 48 B, 48 Br	48 A, 16 B, 16 Br
Aqua/Teal Scraps	¾ yd.	⅓ yd.
	144 A	48 A
Dk. Blue Scraps	⅞ yd.	⅜ yd.
	48 A, 48 C	16 A, 16 C
Navy Print	2¾ yds.	1⅝ yds.
2 borders	4" x 95½"	4" x 55½"
2 borders	4" x 75½"	4" x 55½"
	48 A, 48 C	16 A, 16 C
Bright Blue Print	2⅝ yds.	1½ yds.
2 borders	2" x 88½"	2" x 48½"
2 borders	2" x 68½"	2" x 48½"
binding	2½" x 10 yds.	2½" x 6½ yds.
	48 B, 48 Br	16 B, 16 Br
White/Blue Print	2½ yds.	1⅜ yds.
2 borders	2" x 85½"	2" x 45½"
2 borders	2" x 65½"	2" x 45½"
Lining	5¾ yds.	3⅜ yds.
2 panels	39" x 97"	29" x 57"
Batting	77" x 97"	57" x 57"

Wall Quilt Assembly

(Border corners are mitered after border strips are joined and sewn to quilt.)

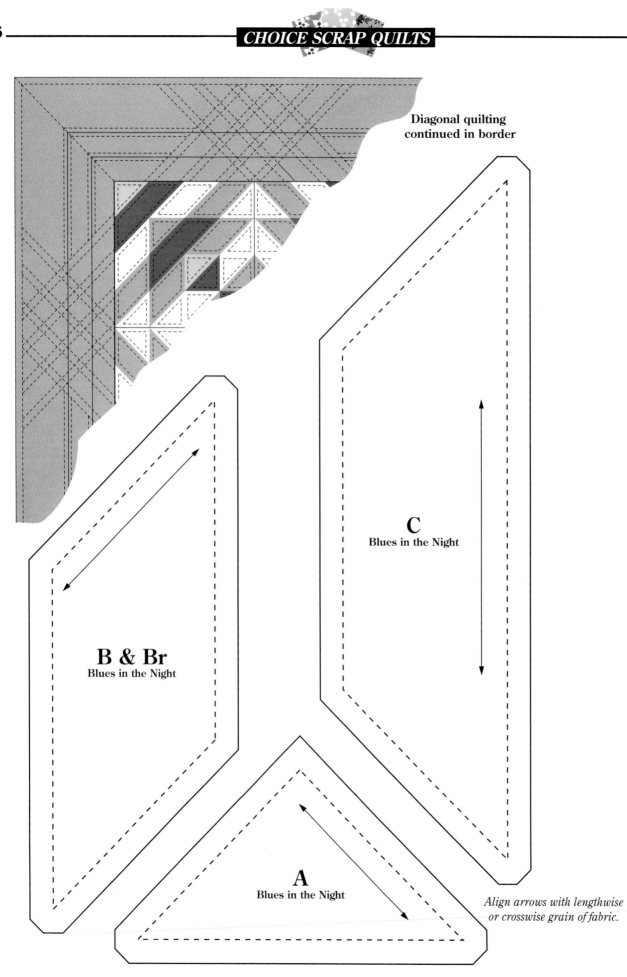

Diagonal quilting
continued in border

C
Blues in the Night

B & Br
Blues in the Night

A
Blues in the Night

*Align arrows with lengthwise
or crosswise grain of fabric.*

Checkpoint

Designed by Caroline Reardon, m
Terri Belke and Maria Reardon (

Cheery rainbow colors in an eas
Patch design make this a perfect
ner's quilt that will delight, especi
you love bold geometrics and high
trasts. A variety of bold prints in n
um-dark and medium-light values f
many color families will help you use up
your scraps! Large patches and square
corners are easy to piece (especially if you
use the strip piecing directions we give
here), and the diagonal setting arrange-
ment adds only a little challenge to the
project. Just check the grain lines on the
corner and side triangles and match
them to the fabric grain. You might want
to make the handsome full-size quilt and
a wall quilt to match. One checkpoint
block with sashing all around and corner
squares would make a decorative pillow.

We tied this quilt with the invisible ty-
ing method described in the General In-
structions, but quilting instructions are
provided in the assembly below.

FULL-SIZE QUILT

Making the Blocks

1 Relax in an area where you can sur-round yourself happily with your fabric scrap collection. Sort your scraps into medium-light and medium-dark piles, grouping by color families–keeping greens together, blues together, and so on. The quilting motifs for patches D and E, and for the border, would show up beautifully on a solid-color fabric or one with a muted design.

If you prefer to piece the quilt with traditional methods, cut out the number of patches as listed in the materials and cutting box. If you wish to use quick-piecing methods, follow the directions given in the instruction box.

The sashes and setting squares are made with high-contrast dark red fabric and cream print fabric. Following the diagrams, make 80 sashes and 49 setting squares. Press all seam allowances toward the red fabric.

Choosing fabrics for blocks will take a little extra time, but will be worth the

fun! Lay your patches for each block out on a flat surface, arranging them until you find the color arrangements that you like. Be sure to place the dark and light patches in the right places to maintain the checkerboard effect. When you are satisfied with the arrangement, join patches to make 32 blocks. If you press all seam allowances toward the dark fabrics, the blocks will go together like a breeze.

Assembling the Quilt Top

2 Take a look at the quilt photo. Notice that this quilt's blocks are arranged in diagonal rows. Don't worry! Because

of all the straight seams in this quilt, the diagonal set is easy to do. Find a large, flat surface and arrange the blocks, sashes, setting squares, side triangles (D's), and corner triangles (E's) into rows, just as you see them in the quilt photo. Move the blocks around until you are pleased with your arrangement of colors and contrasts. Sew the blocks and other parts together into rows. Press the seam allowances toward the sashes. Join the rows.

3 Matching centers, sew the outer borders to the quilt top as explained in the General Instructions. Miter the border corners and trim the excess fabric to leave ¼″ seam allowances.

Taking It to the Finish

4 Press the quilt top and mark the quilting motifs in patches D, E, and the border if desired. (**Note:** Your corner border quilting may appear different than ours, depending on the size of the quilt you make and where you

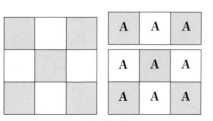

Block Piecing

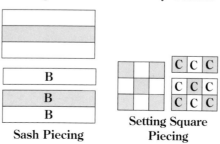

Sash Piecing

Setting Square Piecing

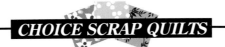

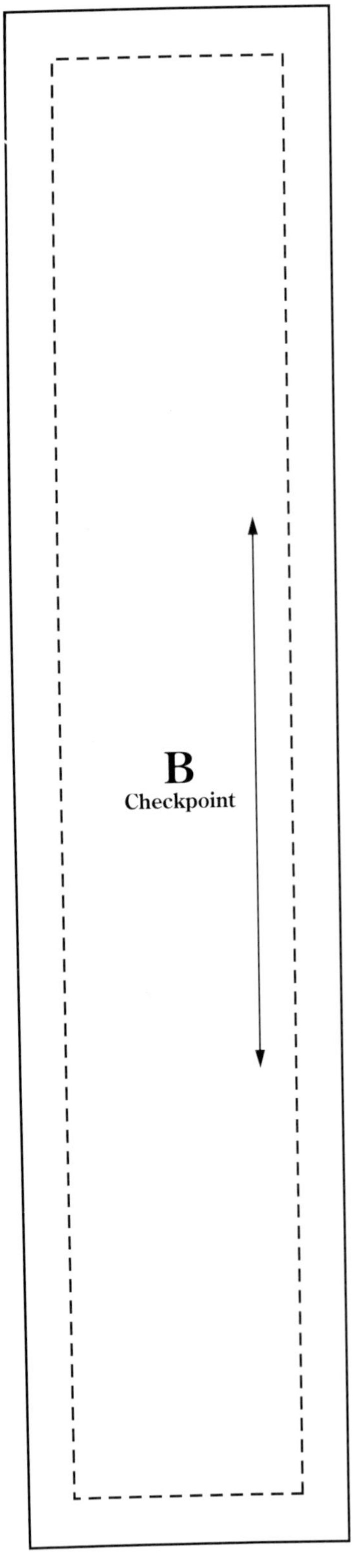
B
Checkpoint

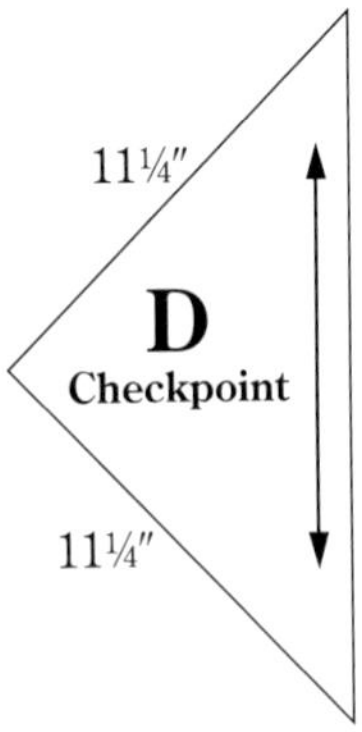
11¼″
D
Checkpoint
11¼″

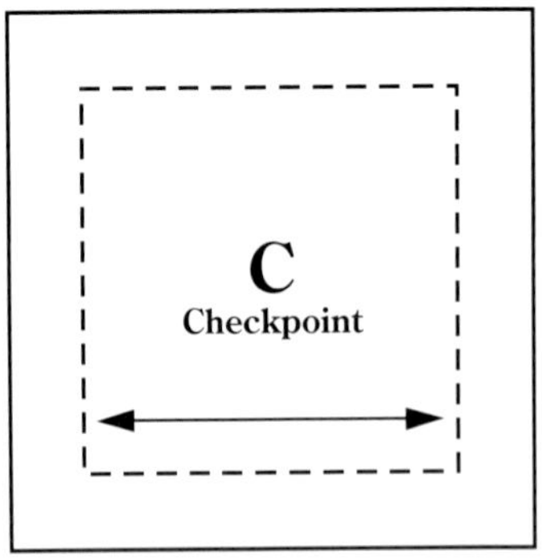
C
Checkpoint

Block Size:	Full-Size Quilt	Wall Quilt
7½″		
Quilt Size:	78″ x 94″	42″ x 42″
Materials and Cutting:		
Tan Print	**1¾ yds.**	**¾ yd.**
	14 D, 4 E	4 D, 4 E
Cream Print	**2⅜ yds.**	**⅝ yd.**
	160 B, 196 C	32 B, 48 C
Dk. Red Print	**3¾ yds.**	**1⅜ yds.**
2 borders	5″ x 96½″	3″ x 44½″
2 borders	5″ x 80½″	3″ x 44½″
binding	2½″ x 10½ yds.	2½″ x 5¼ yds.
	80 B, 245 C	16 B, 60 C
Lt. Scraps	**1 yd.**	**¼ yd.**
	128 A	20 A
Dk. Scraps	**1¼ yds.**	**¼ yd.**
	160 A	25 A
Lining	**5¾ yds.**	**2¾ yds.**
2 panels	41¼″ x 98″	23¼″ x 46″
Batting	**82″ x 98″**	**46″ x 46″**

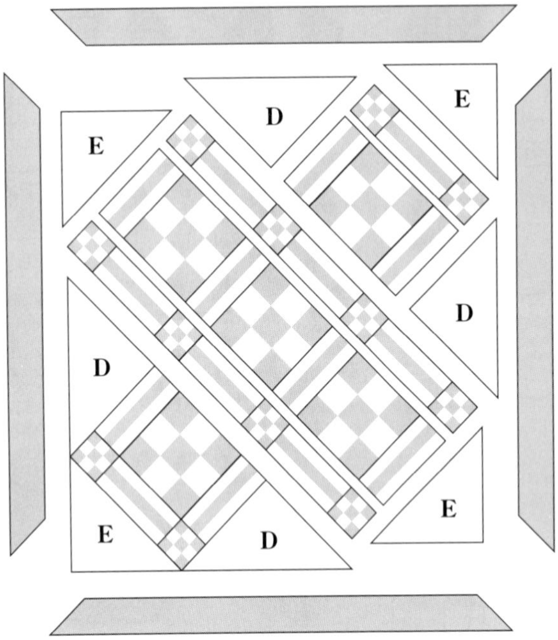
E
D
E
D
D
E
D
E

Wall Quilt Assembly

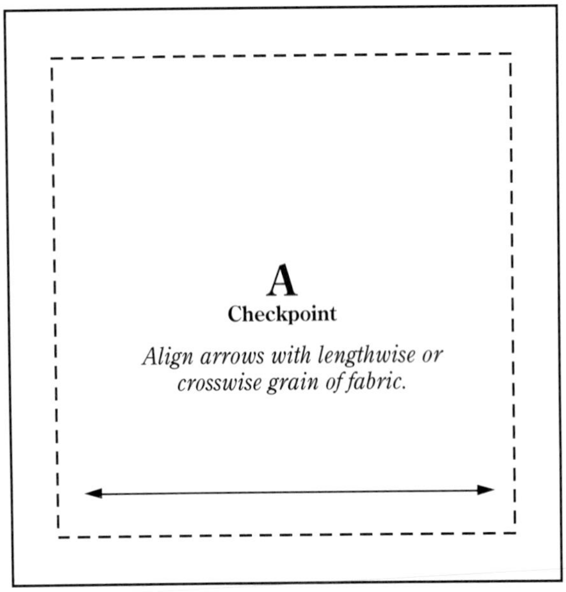
A
Checkpoint
Align arrows with lengthwise or crosswise grain of fabric.

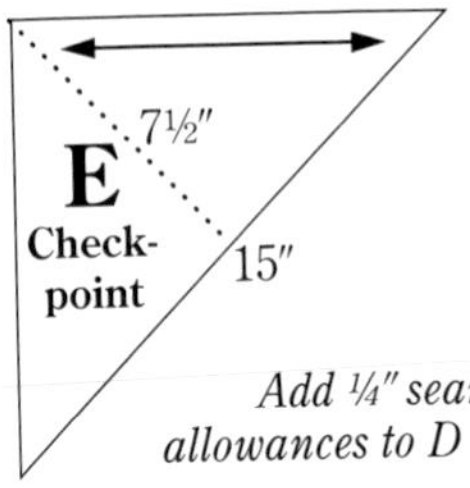
7½″
E
Check-
point
15″

Add ¼″ seam allowances to D and E.

begin marking on the border.) Space the motifs in the border evenly. Sew the lining panels together. Layer the quilt lining, batting, and top. Pin or thread-baste the layers together.

5 We suggest outline quilting ¼″ from the seams of each A patch, inside the patch itself, to accentuate the geometric design. You may want to quilt in-the-ditch around the patches in the sashes and setting squares, so they won't compete for attention with the Nine-Patch blocks. We've designed special motifs for the D and E patches, because those patches are large enough to display detailed quilting motifs. We've also designed a border quilting motif for you, so every part of your quilt will be special.

When you have finished your quilting, apply double-fold binding to finish, as described in the General Instructions. Remember to sign and date your quilt on the back, perhaps with a special label!

WALL QUILT

1 Sort scraps and cut patches as described in Step 1 for the full-size quilt. Referring to the diagrams, make five blocks, 16 sashes and 12 setting squares.

2 Refer to the wall quilt assembly diagram and follow Steps 2 through 5 above to complete the wall quilt. If desired, add a 3″-wide sleeve on the back of the quilt along the top edge for hanging with a rod.

FAST AND EASY STRIP PIECING

The sashes and setting squares in Checkpoint are perfect for strip piecing. Instead of using the cutting instructions in the materials and cutting box for patches B and C, use the following directions. (Wall quilt instructions are given in parentheses.)

Cut borders and binding first. Then cut strips for making the bands, which are several strips sewn together lengthwise. They will take the place of the B and C patches. You will need to cut some strips from the lengthwise and some from the crosswise grain for the most economic use of fabric. Finally, cut the remaining patches.

For the bands for both the sashing and the setting squares, cut 43 (10) 1¾" x 40" strips from the cream fabric and 29 (8) 1¾" x 40" strips from the red fabric. Sew a red strip between two cream strips to make a band 1 as in Fig. 1. Make a total of 19 (4) band 1's. Press seam allowances toward the red fabric.

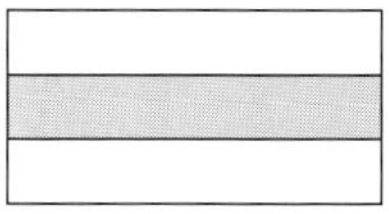

Sew a cream strip between two red ones to make a band 2 as in Fig. 2. Make a total of five (2) band 2's. Press seam allowances toward red fabric.

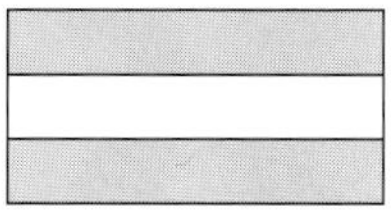

To determine the cut length of the sashes, measure the width of several of your blocks. The blocks should be 8" from raw edge to raw edge. Cut sashes the length of your blocks.

For the setting squares, cut the remaining band 1's into 49 (12) segments that are each 1¾" wide. See Fig. 3. From band 2's, cut 98 (24) segments that are 1¾" wide. There will be leftover material from the band 2's after segments are cut. Make 49 (12) setting squares using chain piecing as described here.

Chain Piecing for Setting Squares

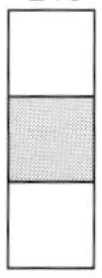

If you are sewing your quilt by machine, you can assemble the setting-square rows by chain piecing them, a fast and efficient technique.

If you look at the quilt photo, you can see that each setting square has three rows (made by cutting strip-pieced bands into segments), and the outer two rows are alike. Place all red/cream/red rows in one pile

and the cream/red/cream rows in another. Pick up one row from each pile and sew them together, matching seams, but don't cut the threads. Instead, continue sewing for a few stitches to make a chain of threads beyond the edge of the fabric. Then pick up the first two rows for the next square, sew them together, and make a thread chain at the edge as before. In other words, sew only the first two rows of every square, all held together in a long chain (Fig. 4).

Don't cut them apart yet. Go back to the first "square" in the chain and add on its third row. Again make a chain at the fabric's edge and add a row to the second square and so on. When you are finished, all of the setting squares will be connected by two little thread chains (Fig. 5). The squares can then be cut apart and pressed before you add them to your quilt.

Fig. 1   Fig. 2

1¾"

Fig. 3

Fig. 4

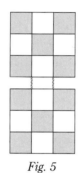

Fig. 5

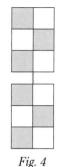

Checkpoint Border Quilting

E

D

Star Twirler

Designed and made by Keiko Hirabayashi

Circles combined with eight-pointed stars and traditional four-patch blocks are the design elements that make this lovely quilt a delight for anyone who enjoys working with color value. The illusion of curved seams makes this quilt look more difficult to make than it is. The quilt is made of only one block, which is quite easy to piece, but thanks to different shading combinations, it looks like two!

The design was inspired by the pattern Judy in Arabia by Jeffrey Gutcheon for The Quilt Design Workbook *in 1976. Star Twirler was first pictured in the pages of* Patchwork Quilt Tsushin, *a Japanese magazine that often features modern variations of traditional blocks.*

WALL QUILT

Choosing and Preparing Fabrics

1 To make a quilt similar to the one in the photo, the most important consideration in fabric choice is to keep the dark fabrics considerably darker than all the light and medium-light fabrics. Nearly any color combination would be successful. Prewash your fabrics. Damp dry and press them. Sort the fabrics into piles of light, medium-light, and dark prints.

Sewing the Blocks

2 Study the photo of the quilt in the color pages to see how the scraps are arranged. In one block, all four C patches are cut from the same print. However, in the next block, each C is different. The quiltmaker used this random placement of prints to give the quilt a true scrap look. Since you might use a fabric only once in the entire quilt, you can use even the smallest bits of fabric in your stash. As long as you keep the dark fabrics in the correct positions in the two block colorations, the light patches will form the overall design.

Prepare templates and mark the fabric as explained in the General Instructions. Cut the patches needed. Using the block diagrams and quilt photo for guidance, make one Y block and one Z block. The only difference between them is the placement of color, so it is helpful to make one of each for color reference as you sew the rest of the blocks. Make a total of 28 Y blocks and 28 Z blocks.

Assembling the Quilt Top

3 Beginning with a Y block, alternately join four Y and three Z blocks for the odd-numbered rows. Make four rows like this. Beginning with a Z block, alternately join four Z and three Y blocks for an even-numbered row. Make four rows like this. Stitch rows together, alternating types.

4 To easily add the multiple mitered borders, read about sewing multiple plain borders in the General Instructions. Add the borders and miter the seams.

Taking It to the Finish

5 Lightly press the quilt and mark the border quilting motif in the borders as shown in the border quilting diagram. Clip any threads that are hanging from the back. Sew the lining panels together. Layer the quilt lining, batting, and top. Baste the layers, following the directions in the General Instructions.

6 This quilt would look nice with embroidery-floss ties centered in each A and C patch. If you prefer to quilt it by hand or machine, quilt in-the-ditch around the B/Br, C, and D patches. Quilt ¼" from the edges of the A patches. Quilt the outer border with the border motif we've provided, or quilt ¼" from the border seams. Apply double-fold binding to finish.

☐ Light Scraps　▨ Medium Light Scraps　■ Dark Scraps

Block Y　　**Block Z**　　**Blocks Y & Z Piecing**

Block Size:	Wall	Pillow
6″	**Quilt**	
Quilt Size:	49″ x 55″	20″ x 20″
Quilt Requires:	28 Y blocks	5 Y blocks
	28 Z blocks	4 Z blocks
Materials and Cutting:		
Lt. Scraps	**2⅛ yds.**	**⅜ yd.**
	224 B, 224 Br,	36 B, 36 Br,
	224 D	36 D
Med. Lt. Scraps	**1¼ yds.**	**¼ yd.**
	112 A, 112 C,	18 A, 20 C,
	112 D	16 D
Dk. Scraps	**1¼ yds.**	**¼ yd.**
	112 A, 112 C,	18 A, 16 C,
	112 D	20 D
Turquoise Solid	**1⅝ yds.**	**None**
2 borders	1″ x 51½″	
2 borders	1″ x 45½″	
Royal Blue Print	**1¾ yds.**	**¼ yd.**
2 borders	3½″ x 57½″	1½″ x 22½″
2 borders	3½″ x 51½″	1½″ x 22½″
Navy Solid	**½ yd.**	**None**
binding	2½″ x 6¾ yds.	
Lining	**3⅛ yds.**	See pillow
2 panels	30″ x 53″	backing information below.
Batting	**53″ x 59″**	**24″ x 24″**
Pillow Stuffing		**1½ lbs.**
or pillow form		20″ x 20″
Pillow Inner Lining		**¾ yd.**
1 panel		24″ x 24″
Pillow Backing		**¾ yd.**
1 panel		24″ x 24″

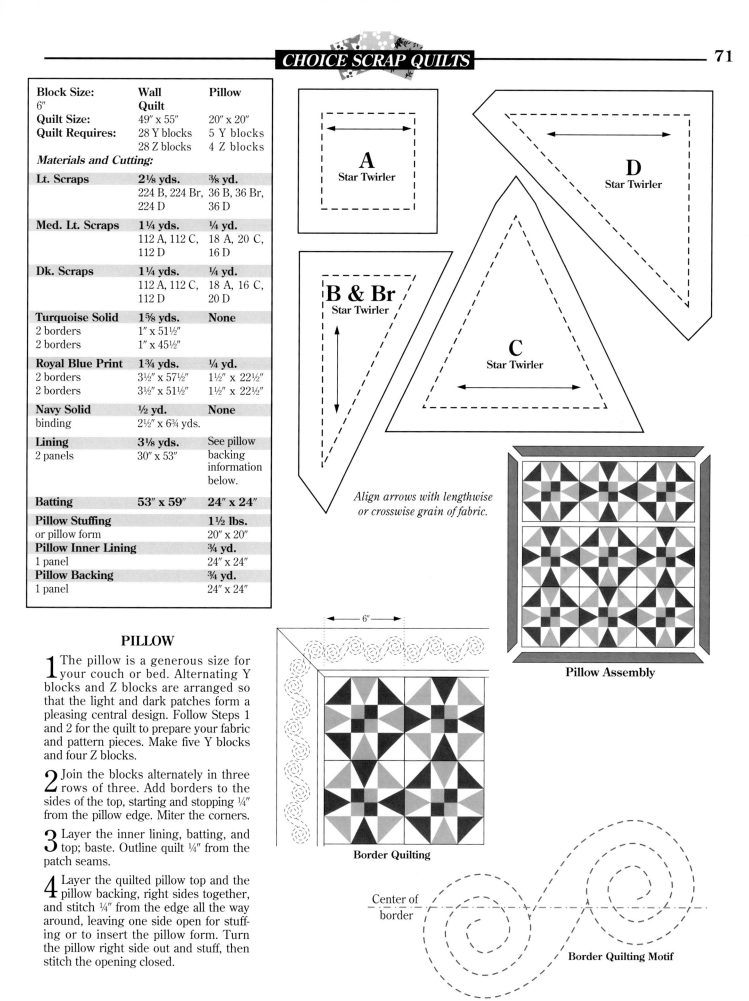

A — Star Twirler

B & Br — Star Twirler

C — Star Twirler

D — Star Twirler

Align arrows with lengthwise or crosswise grain of fabric.

Pillow Assembly

Border Quilting

Center of border

Border Quilting Motif

PILLOW

1 The pillow is a generous size for your couch or bed. Alternating Y blocks and Z blocks are arranged so that the light and dark patches form a pleasing central design. Follow Steps 1 and 2 for the quilt to prepare your fabric and pattern pieces. Make five Y blocks and four Z blocks.

2 Join the blocks alternately in three rows of three. Add borders to the sides of the top, starting and stopping ¼″ from the pillow edge. Miter the corners.

3 Layer the inner lining, batting, and top; baste. Outline quilt ¼″ from the patch seams.

4 Layer the quilted pillow top and the pillow backing, right sides together, and stitch ¼″ from the edge all the way around, leaving one side open for stuffing or to insert the pillow form. Turn the pillow right side out and stuff, then stitch the opening closed.

Country Still Life

Designed by Mary Leman Austin and Theresa Eisinger, made by Lucy Brown and Carolee Miller

A basket, pitcher, and posies are arranged in a country still life to form the centerpiece of this easy-to-make wall quilt. The blue-and-white checkerboard border adds a touch of homespun charm, and the floral border adds lively color that sparks the whole composition.

We recommend this pattern to beginners, particularly in the wall-quilt size. The appliqué motifs are simple shapes that a new quiltmaker will find quite manageable, especially with the help of the freezer-paper appliqué directions. The patchwork portion of the quilt couldn't be easier to piece, either by hand or machine.

The twin-size quilt is easy also; it just takes longer to complete. It is made of 12 blocks framed with sashing strips and setting squares. The outer border has no appliqué.

Whether you decide on the wall or twin size, you will have a lovely folk-art quilt to display and enjoy.

WALL QUILT

Choosing and Cutting the Fabrics

1 We used the same two fabrics for the squares in the checkerboard border, but if you want an even scrappier look, you could use a variety of dark blue prints and white-on-white prints for the checked border. Our quilt uses many different prints for the flowers. You can make them in any colors you like. There are many interesting prints that would make a lovely pitcher. We found a print that makes the pitcher look like painted pottery.

When working with the light blue print, cut the borders first, then cut the four M patches. Cut the other patches from your chosen scraps.

Appliquéing the Center

2 To help you in positioning the appliqué patches, fold the background patch A in half lengthwise to find the center. Align the center of A with the center dot on the full-size pattern, having the bottom of the D patch (the basket) aligned with the bottom *sewing line* of A. Lightly trace the basket, pitcher, and flowers on the A patch.

3 To prepare the fabric patches for appliqué, turn under the 3/16″ allowances on patches C–L and baste. (More detailed instructions for appliqué are in the General Instructions.) Note that the bottom edges of the pitcher and the basket are stitched into the seam between the A and B patches, so do *not*

turn under their straight bottom edges.

4 You will need many short lengths of bias stripping for the stems in the center and in the border. It is more efficient to make a few long bias strips and cut them to the length you need. Make bias stripping for stems in this manner: Fold bias strips in half lengthwise with wrong sides together. Sew 1/4″ from the *folded* edge. Trim close to the stitching. Press the strip flat, keeping the seam allowance concealed on the underneath side. Cut the strip as needed for the stems.

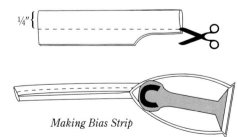

Making Bias Strip

5 Position, pin, and blindstitch the stems, pitcher, basket, leaves, and flowers in alphabetical order on A. Note that the red flower at the bottom of the pitcher extends over the seam between

the A and B patches, so set that flower aside until it is needed. Baste the bottom edges of C and D patches in place so that they will be stitched into the seam.

6 If you enjoy embellishing appliqué with embroidery, here is your chance to show off your needlework skills. The full-size patterns show french knots circling and clustering around the flower centers, but you might also consider adding a row or two of outline stitches around the centers or embroidering lines radiating from the center of the blossoms. Small seed beads stitched in place of the french knots would add a sparkle to your wall quilt as well.

Assembling the Center Block

7 Now you are ready to assemble the parts to make the center block. Stitch the long edge of B patch to the bottom edge of A, catching the bottom edges of the basket and pitcher in the seam. Press the seam allowances toward the B patch. Stitch an M patch to each corner to make the center square. You can appliqué and embroider the bottom red flower that you set aside earlier.

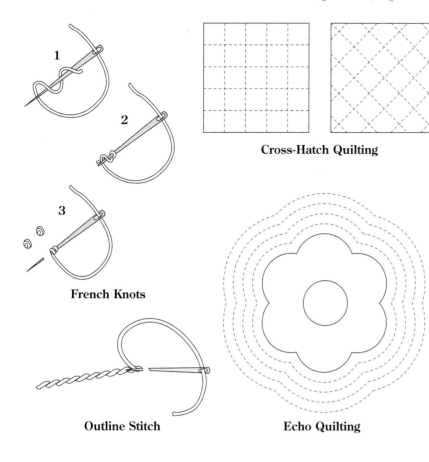

1
2
3

French Knots

Outline Stitch

Cross-Hatch Quilting

Echo Quilting

Block Size:	Wall	Twin-Size
15″	Quilt	Quilt
Quilt Size:	35″ x 35″	67″ x 83″
Materials and Cutting:		
White Print	¼ yd.	¾ yd.
	5 I, 120 N	12 I, 360 N
White/Yellow Print	½ yd.	2 yds.
	1 A	12 A
Yellow Print	⅛ yd.	⅜ yd.
	1 B	12 B
Yellow Scraps	⅛ yd.	⅓ yd.
	5 H, 2 I,	12 H, 24 I,
	1 K, 1 L	12 K, 12 L
Gold Print	⅓ yd.	2½ yds.
2 borders	1½″ x 33½″	1½″ x 81½″
2 borders	1½″ x 33½″	1½″ x 65½″
	1 D, 4 O	12 D, 31 O
Lt. Blue Print	⅞ yd.	2½ yds.
2 borders	5½″ x 33½″	5½″ x 81½″
2 borders	5½″ x 33½″	5½″ x 65½″
	4 M	48 M
Med. Blue Print	¼ yd.	½ yd.
	1 C	12 C
Dk. Blue Print	⅝ yd.	1¼ yds.
binding	2½″ x 4¼ yds.	2½″ x 9⅛ yds.
	120 N	360 N
Blue Scraps	⅛ yd.	⅜ yd.
	1 H, 5 I,	12 H, 60 I,
	1 J, 1 K	12 J, 12 K
Green Solid	⅜ yd.	⅓ yd.
bias strip	1″ x 1¾ yds.	1″ x 2⅓ yds.
	54 E	72 E
Red/Pink Scraps	⅜ yd.	½ yd.
	18 F, 18 G,	24 F, 24 G,
	1 H, 1 I, 8 N	12 H, 12 I,
		24 N
Lining	1¼ yds.	5⅛ yds.
1 panel	39″ x 39″	
2 panels		36″ x 87″
Batting	39″ x 39″	71″ x 87″
Embroidery Floss: red, medium blue		

Border measurements are the exact length needed plus seam allowances.

8 Fold a gold O patch and the center block in half to find the center of each and lightly crease the folds. Matching the centers, sew an O patch to two opposite sides of the quilt. Sew a red N patch to each end of the remaining short gold strips. Match centers and align the seams of the gold strips with the seams of the block; sew borders to the remaining sides.

Making the Checkerboard Border

9 It is important to sew all the white and blue squares with accurate ¼″ seam allowances so that the pieced border will fit nicely. Instructions for checking the accuracy of your seam allowances are in the General Instructions under "Machine Piecing." The border is simple to make–just follow the steps one by one.

Join nine white N's alternately with eight blue N's. Make two rows like this. Join nine blue N's alternately with eight white N's. Join these three rows to make a checkerboard strip. Sew to one side of the quilt. Repeat for the opposite side. Join 12 blue N's alternately with 11 white N's. Make two rows like this. Join 12 white N's alternately with 11 blue N's. Join these three rows to make a checkerboard strip. Sew to the top of the quilt. Repeat for the bottom of the quilt.

Adding the Outer Borders

10 Feel free to arrange the stems, leaves, and flowers in the outer border as you like. Remember that the borders will be mitered, so don't place the flowers too close to the end. If you prefer, you can position and appliqué the flowers *after* the borders are sewn to the quilt and the corners are mitered.

If you plan to position the flowers as shown in the quilt, follow these steps. To find the center of the blue border strips, fold the borders in half lengthwise and crosswise and lightly crease the folds. Position the patches as shown on page 76. Center a yellow H patch in the middle of the border. Referring to the border diagram, position other flowers so that their bottom edges are 4½″ and 9½″ from the center fold. Position the leaves and bias strips, curving the stems as in the illustration. Blindstitch in place. Embroider and embellish the flowers as described in Step 6.

11 If you have not already sewn the wide blue borders to the quilt, do so now. Miter the corners and trim the excess to leave ¼″ seam allowances. Add the gold borders and red N patches the same way you did in Step 8.

Taking It to the Finish

12 Mark the quilting motifs in the M patches. Sew the lining panels together. Layer and baste the lining, batting, and quilt top as explained in the General Instructions.

13 Quilt the motifs in the M patches. Simple quilting that follows the shapes of the appliqué patches and the checkerboard border is the only other quilting that you need. Quilt around all the appliqués and ¼″ from the seams of

the checkerboard. If you want more quilting, fill in the background behind the appliqués with quilting lines that echo the shapes of the appliqués, or with a filler of cross-hatched lines.

14 Apply double-fold binding to finish. If desired, add a 3″-wide sleeve on the back of the quilt along the top edge for hanging with a rod. Be sure to label your quilt with your name, the date, and place.

TWIN-SIZE QUILT

1 Nearly any color scheme will work with this quilt. Choose strongly contrasting fabrics for the checkerboard border and a tone-on-tone print for the sashes that frame the blocks. (Tone-on-tone refers to a fabric print that "reads" like a one-color solid.) Follow the directions for the wall quilt to choose and prepare fabric and cut the patches.

2 Follow Steps 2 through 7 for the wall quilt to make 12 appliquéd blocks.

3 The blocks are surrounded by sashing strips that frame them. To make a block row, alternately join three appliquéd blocks with four gold sashes

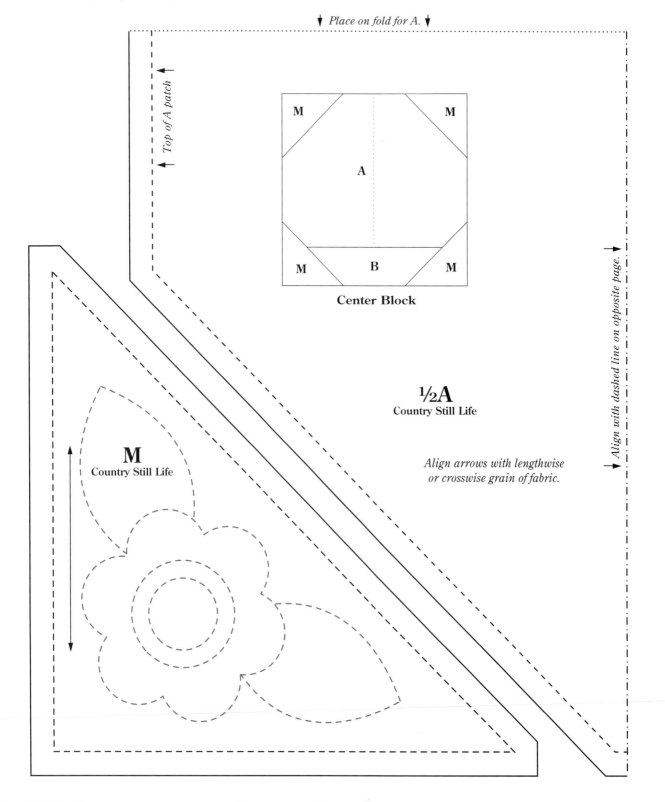

▼ Place on fold for A. ▼

Top of A patch

Center Block

M   M

A

M   B   M

½A
Country Still Life

Align arrows with lengthwise or crosswise grain of fabric.

M
Country Still Life

Align with dashed line on opposite page.

(O patches). Make four block rows. To make a sash row, alternately join four red setting squares (N's) with three gold O patches. Make five sash rows. Matching the seams, join the rows, alternating the block and the sash rows.

4 To make the checked pieced border, join 33 white N's alternately with 32 blue N's to make a row. Make two rows like this. Join 33 blue N's alternately with 32 white N's. Join these three rows to make a checkerboard strip. Sew to one side of the quilt. Repeat for the opposite side. Join 28 blue N's alternately with 27 white N's. Make two rows like this. Join 28 white N's alternately with 27 blue N's. Join these three rows to make a checkerboard strip. Sew to the top of the quilt. Repeat for the bottom of the quilt.

5 Sew the blue borders to the quilt, mitering corners and trimming the excess to leave ¼" seam allowances.

6 Sew the long gold print border strips to the sides of the quilt. Sew a red N patch to the remaining gold strips, and sew to the top and bottom of the quilt.

7 Refer to the wall quilt directions to finish.

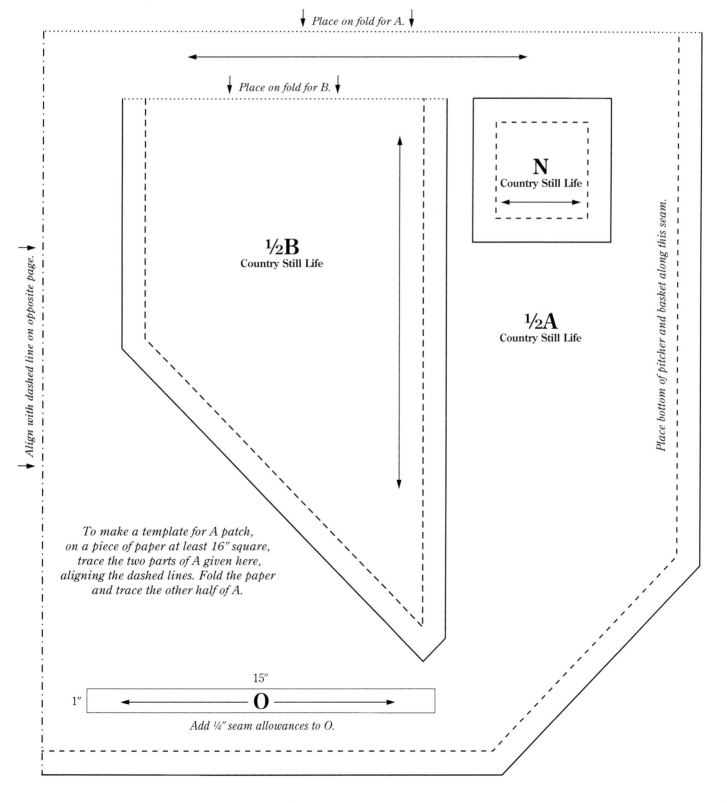

Place on fold for A.

Place on fold for B.

N
Country Still Life

½B
Country Still Life

½A
Country Still Life

Align with dashed line on opposite page.

Place bottom of pitcher and basket along this seam.

To make a template for A patch, on a piece of paper at least 16" square, trace the two parts of A given here, aligning the dashed lines. Fold the paper and trace the other half of A.

15"

1"

O

Add ¼" seam allowances to O.

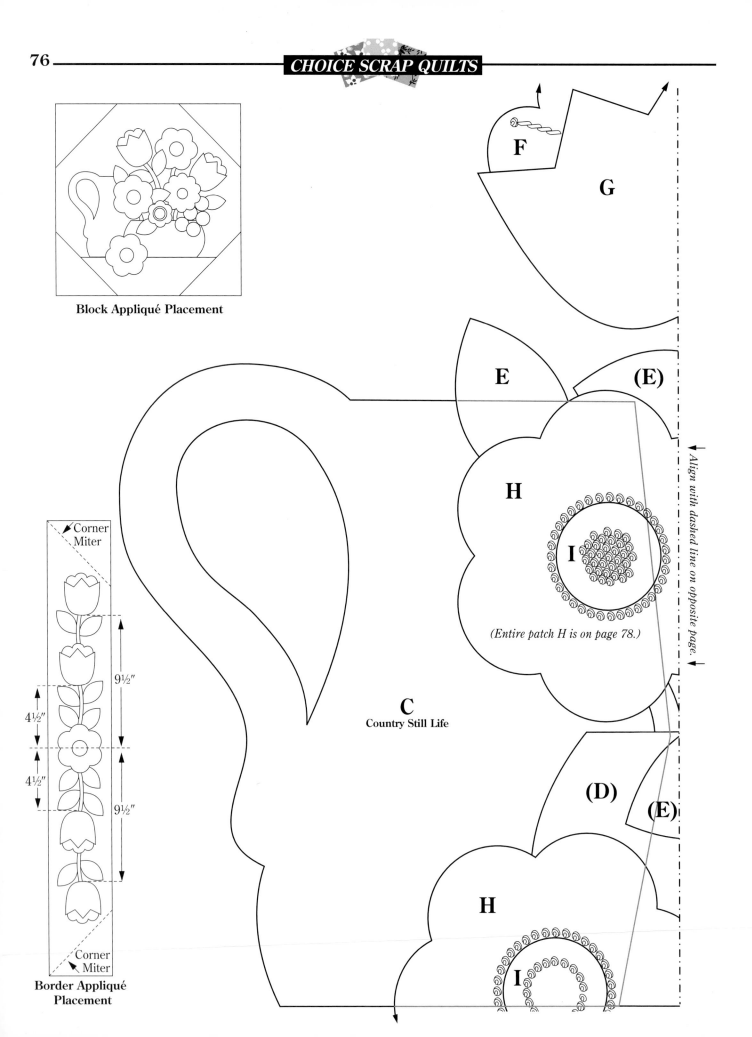

Block Appliqué Placement

F

G

E

(E)

H

I

(Entire patch H is on page 78.)

C
Country Still Life

Align with dashed line on opposite page.

(D)

(E)

H

I

Corner Miter

9½″

4½″

4½″

9½″

Corner Miter

Border Appliqué Placement

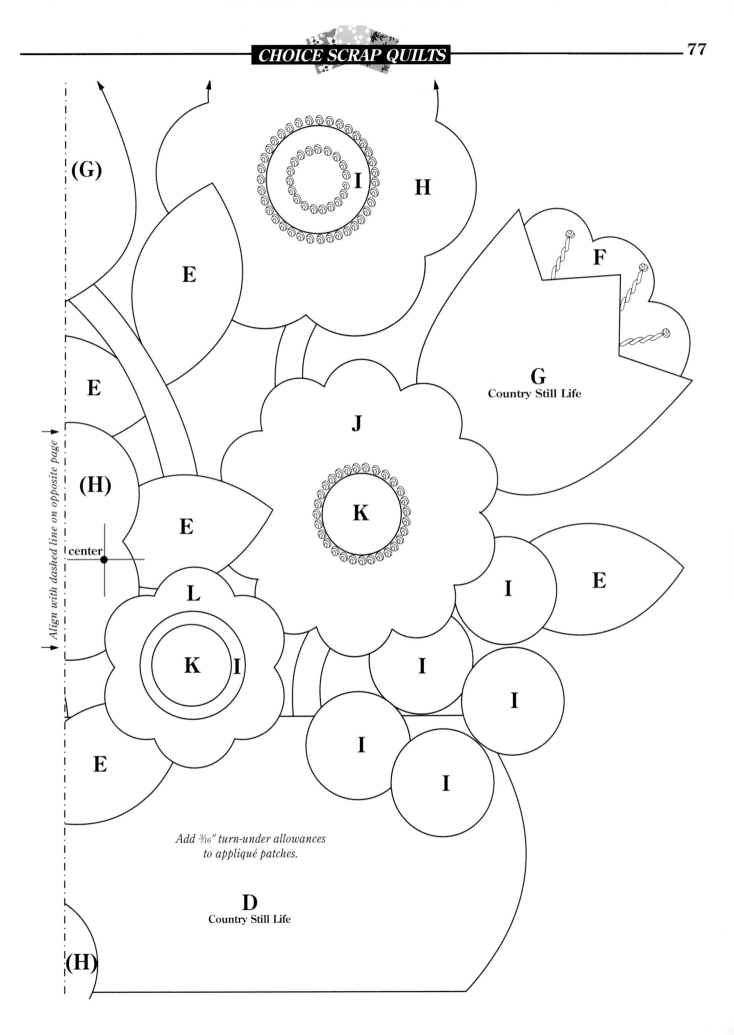

(G)

(H)

(H)

center

E

E

E

E

E

E

L

K

I

K

J

I

I

I

I

I

I

I

H

F

G
Country Still Life

Align with dashed line on opposite page

*Add ³⁄₁₆" turn-under allowances
to appliqué patches.*

D
Country Still Life

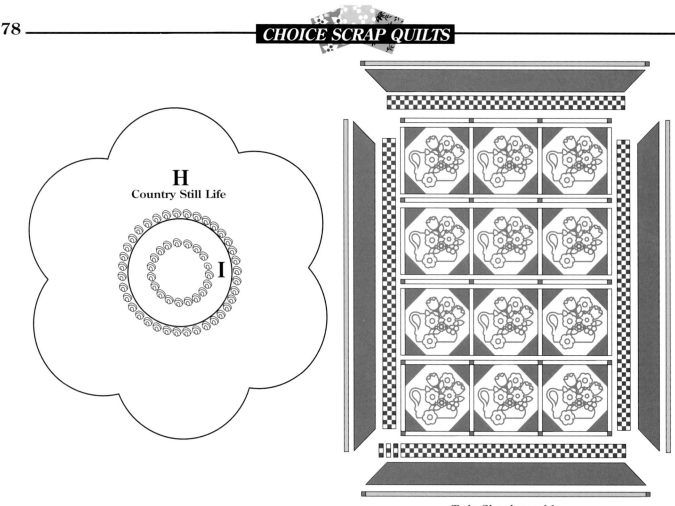

H
Country Still Life

I

Twin-Size Assembly

FREEZER-PAPER APPLIQUÉ

The simple flowers and leaves are repeated many times in this quilt. The use of freezer paper as a foundation will help you to make all the flowers the same size and shape.

Position a piece of freezer paper sticky side down on the full-size pattern and trace a motif. Cut out the paper with no turn-under allowances.

To make a cardboard template, with a warm iron, press the sticky side of the paper shape to lightweight cardboard, and cut the cardboard out with no turn-under allowances. Use this sturdy template to make more freezer-paper templates since you will need one for each patch. If the patch is symmetrical (flowers, leaves, and basket), the cardboard template can be placed on the dull side of the freezer paper to trace. If the patch is directional (the pitcher) turn the cardboard template *over* to place on the dull side of the freezer paper. Trace around the cardboard template on the dull side of the

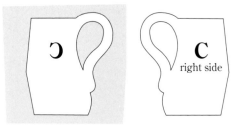

Turn over directional templates to place on the dull side of the freezer paper.

freezer paper to make a paper template for each patch in the quilt. Stack the freezer paper to cut several at a time.

Press a paper template sticky side down on the *wrong* side of the fabric. Cut out the fabric patch with a ³⁄₁₆″ turn-under allowance measured by eye. Again, you can cut several fabric patches at one time. Press a paper template to the wrong side of each fabric patch.

Press the fabric turn-under allowance to the back side of the patch with an iron (see figure), or use a needle to turn

the allowance under as you stitch the patch in place. Clip into curves if needed. As you turn the allowance under, the freezer-paper template will help you create clean, crisp edges. Position, pin, and blindstitch each patch on the background (see figure below).

When you have an inch or so of stitching left on the patch, pull the freezer paper out and complete the stitching.

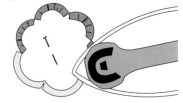

Pressing turn-under allowance

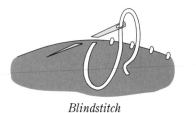

Blindstitch

Columbia Star

Designed and made by Diana Voyer

This challenging and wonderful star quilt fairly dances with energy and fun! Any colors of the spectrum would be terrific as long as you use a range of fairly high-contrast light, medium, and dark scraps. Sparkling dark and medium diamonds make six-pointed stars, surrounded by light diamonds to form hexagon and half-hexagon blocks. Red triangles float along the top and bottom, and dark borders serve as a frame. English paper piecing is one good way to join these colorful blocks, and we provide instructions.

FULL-SIZE QUILT

Cutting and Sewing Blocks

1 The first thing to do is to sort your scraps into lights, mediums, and darks. You may wish to plan on using one colorway for the mediums in each block and another colorway for the darks in each block as we did, or you may choose to mix up your colorways for a totally scrappy look. To keep the sparkling effect of the stars, though, you will want to alternate the medium and dark diamonds in each star and keep the set-in diamonds of your hexagon block light in color.

Accurate piecing is essential for hexagonal blocks such as these, and with hand piecing you can achieve this with ease. Machine piecing is not recommended. When marking for hand piecing, be sure to place the template face down on the wrong side of the fabric and trace around the template (this will be your sewing line). The materials and cutting box lists the number of patches you will need to cut for either the full-size or the wall quilt.

2 Now look at the piecing diagram for block Y. Experiment with laying out your dark, medium, and light A's as in the drawing. When you like what you see, sew one Y block. To sew a Y block, join three dark print A's alternately with three medium print A's to form a six-pointed star. Set in light print A's between the points of the star as shown. (See the General Instructions for details of sewing set-in patches or read the instructions on page 81 for English paper piecing.) Make a total of 83 Y blocks.

3 Next, look at the diagram for the Z block. The Z blocks look like half of a Y block and are used along the sides of the quilt. Note that some of the Z blocks use two dark A's and one light A, while others use two light A's and one dark A. To sew a Z block, lay out your

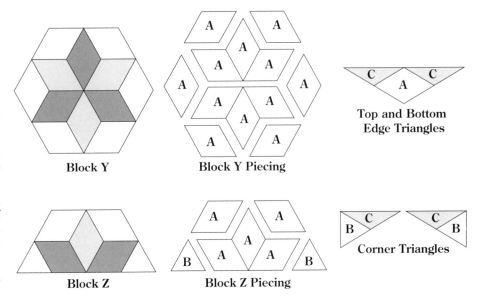

patches as you did for Block Y until you are satisfied with your choices. Sew one Z block. Make a total of 10 Z blocks.

4 The edge triangles are made with two red C's and one light A. Refer-

ring to the edge triangle diagram, make 14. The corner triangles are made with one red C and one light B. Make two of each kind of corner triangle, noting the placement of the B patch.

Block Y

Block Y Piecing

Top and Bottom Edge Triangles

Block Z

Block Z Piecing

Corner Triangles

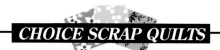

Block Size:	Full-Size Quilt	Wall Quilt
7½″		
Quilt Size:	70½″ x 84⅛″	40½″ x 45⅛″
Quilt Requires:	83 Y Blocks	18 Y Blocks
	10 Z Blocks	4 Z Blocks
Materials and Cutting:		
Lt. Print Scraps	**3 yds.**	**⅞ yd.**
	532 A, 24 B	122 A, 12 B
Med. Print Scraps	**1½ yds.**	**½ yd.**
	264 A	60 A
Dk. Print Scraps	**1½ yds.**	**½ yd.**
	264 A	60 A
Red Print	**2⅝ yds.**	**1½ yds.**
2 borders	4¾″ x 86⅝″	4¾″ x 47⅝″
2 borders	4¾″ x 73″	4¾″ x 43″
	32 C	16 C
Dk. Blue Solid	**2⅜ yds.**	**1¼ yds.**
2 borders	1½″ x 78⅛″	1½″ x 39⅛″
2 borders	1½″ x 64½″	1½″ x 34½″
binding	2½″ x 9⅜ yds.	2½″ x 5⅜ yds.
Lining	**5¼ yds.**	**2⅝ yds.**
2 panels	37¾″ x 88⅛″	25″ x 44½″
Batting	**74½″x88⅛″**	**44½″x49⅛″**

Assembling the Quilt Top

5 Look carefully at the quilt assembly diagram for the wall quilt. You'll see that the blocks are arranged in diagonal rows, which is necessary because of the shape of the blocks. Follow the diagram as you go.

Find a large flat surface and arrange the blocks as you see them in the wall quilt diagram and in the photo. Rearrange your blocks as necessary until you are satisfied with your color placement. Join Y blocks end to end as follows: three diagonal rows of 11 Y blocks each, two diagonal rows of nine Y blocks each, two diagonal rows of seven Y blocks each, two diagonal rows of five Y blocks each, and two diagonal rows of three Y blocks each; add Z blocks, edge triangles, and corner triangles along the outer edges. Lay the rows out in the order of assembly. The wall quilt assembly diagram will aid you with this. Then sew the diagonal rows together, paying particular attention at the set-in corners so the quilt will lie flat.

Adding the Borders

6 Fold a short blue solid border in half to find the center. Do the same for one short red border. Then, sew one short blue solid border to one short red print border along their long sides, matching centers. Fold the quilt in half both directions to find the centers of the sides. Now, take the red and blue borders that you have joined and place the blue border next to the top row of blocks in the quilt, matching centers. Sew the borders to the top. Repeat this process for the other short blue border and red print border, matching centers and sewing them to the bottom of the quilt.

Repeat this process for the side borders, using the long blue solid borders and red print borders, matching centers as described above and joining them to the quilt sides. Miter the corners as described for multiple borders in the General Instructions chapter.

Taking It to the Finish

7 Sew the lining panels together. Layer quilt lining, batting, and top. Pin or thread-baste the layers together.

8 We suggest quilting diagonally from point to point in the light print A's around each star, as shown in the quilting diagram. Quilt diagonal lines 2″ to 3″ apart along the red print outer border, and if you wish, you could quilt in-the-ditch along the blue border. When you have finished quilting, apply double-fold binding to finish. Remember to sign and date your quilt on the back.

WALL QUILT

1 Choose your fabric, cut the patches, and sew one Y block and one Z block as described in Step 1 of the full-size assembly instructions. (Be sure to refer to the materials and cutting box for the correct number of patches to cut for the wall quilt.) Make a total of 18 Y blocks and four Z blocks. Make six edge triangles and two of each kind of corner triangle.

2 Referring to the wall quilt assembly diagram, sew Y blocks end to end as follows: two diagonal rows of five Y blocks each and two diagonal rows of three Y blocks each.

Join rows of Y blocks as shown in the wall quilt assembly diagram, adding Z blocks, edge triangles, and corner triangles along the outer edges as shown.

3 Follow Steps 3 through 8 of the instructions for the full-size quilt assembly.

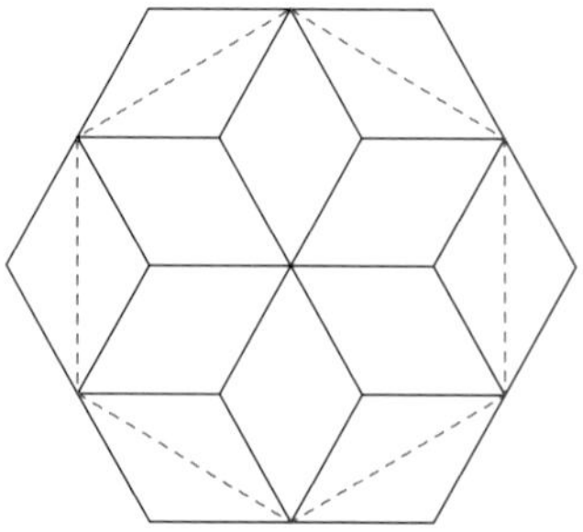

Y Block Quilting

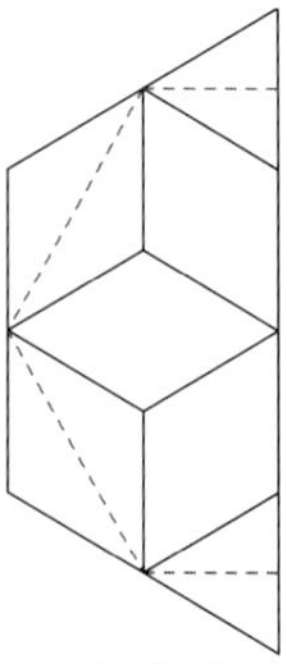

Z Block Quilting

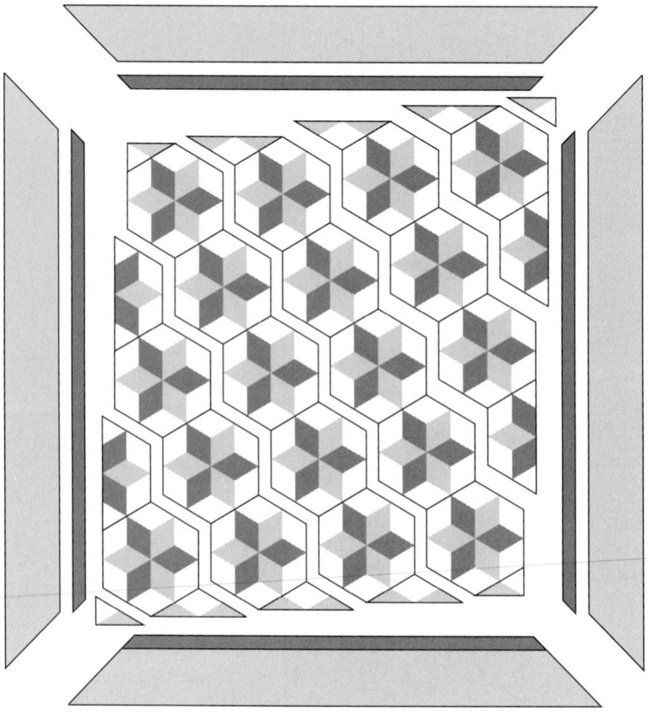

Wall Quilt Assembly

ENGLISH PAPER PIECING

You may find English paper piecing, a traditional hand-piecing technique which originated in England long ago, your method of choice for joining the patches in this quilt. This method virtually guarantees a perfect fit.

A lightweight card or paper template must be cut the exact finished size for each patch in the quilt. The template should *not* include seam allowances. Any good, heavy writing paper or something similar may be used. Do not use newspaper, because the ink will rub off on your fabric. (Quilt stores and mail-order quilting supply sources frequently carry precut paper templates in many standard sizes of hexagon and diamond shapes.)

Cut out fabric patches with seam allowances included. Center a paper template on the *wrong* side of the patch, fold the seam allowance snugly over the edge of the template, and baste with a neutral-color thread. It is not necessary to use a backstitch or to knot the thread when basting. As each edge of the patch is turned down, the fold of the fabric should wrap precisely around the edge of the paper template to make sharp, crisp corners.

Two basted diamond patches joined with overcast stitch

invisible stitches. When the two patches are joined, open them out and finger press the seam flat. (Seam allowances are *not* pressed to one side as for the traditional hand-piecing technique.) Sew a second dark diamond to the other side of the medium diamond. This completes half of the star.

Complete the other half of the star by joining two medium diamonds and one

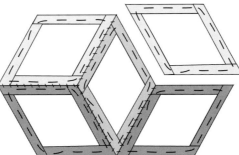

Diamonds joined with overcast stitch, and inserted patch

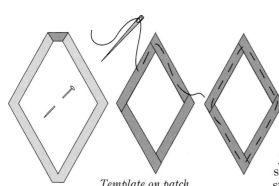

Template on patch, basting, and basted patch

After all your patches have been basted, place a dark A diamond on a medium A diamond, right sides together. Using a single strand of thread in a color that matches one of the patches, sew in an overcast stitch, catching just two or three threads from each patch and trying not to catch the paper in the stitching. Use tiny overcast stitches to join the patches. Fine cotton thread and a fine needle will help you make nearly

dark diamond patch, then join the two halves of the star. Add the six light patches in the angles of the six-pointed star, which are necessary to complete the hexagon block.

Never attempt to turn a corner and join two seams with one thread. Instead, finish off one seam with backstitches, run the thread through to the back side, and cut the thread. Then reposition the patches so the edges of the next seam match precisely before sewing.

Look at the quilt assembly diagram. Choose a corner and begin joining the blocks, continuing until the quilt top is completed (except for the borders).

After the patchwork is finished, remove the basting threads and paper. Add the borders and complete the quilt as described in the assembly instructions for this pattern.

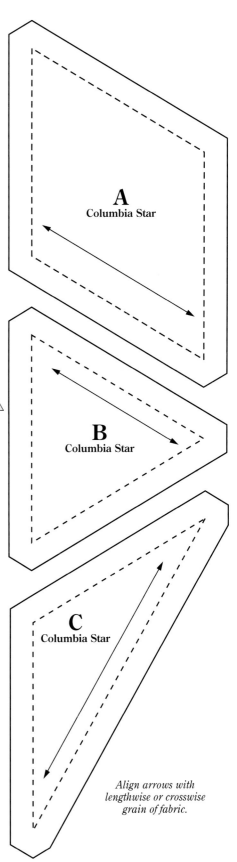

A
Columbia Star

B
Columbia Star

C
Columbia Star

Align arrows with lengthwise or crosswise grain of fabric.

Xanadu

Designed and made by Faye Anderson

A tapestry of warm fall colors enriches this quilt by Faye Anderson. No two blocks use the same combination of prints for the flowers and leaves, and the sashes also are made from a wide variety of scraps. Two floral prints frame the quilt, with Faye's corded edging adding a final touch. For those of you who enjoy appliqué but do not want a bed-size quilt, a very striking wall quilt can be made with just four whole blocks and eight partial blocks.

Faye's quilt was honored at the 1994 American Quilter's Society show in Paducah, Kentucky, with a first prize in the Appliqué, Professional category.

TWIN-SIZE QUILT

Making the Blocks

1 When selecting fabrics, choose very light geometric prints, including subtle plaids and stripes, for the background A patches. The back sides of some fabrics may be light enough to use. The leaves and stems use a range of teals and green prints from medium/light to dark. The flowers and buds are made from a variety of warm colors, including reds, rusts, purples, lavenders, and golds. Each sash is made with three strips (T's), two from green/teal scraps and one from red/gold scraps. The more variety that you use, the richer the quilt will look. Faye used colors that are somewhat muted rather than bright and clear. Follow the suggestions for selecting scrap fabrics in the chapter Working With Scraps.

Once you have chosen your fabrics, cut the borders, binding, bias for stems, and patches listed in the materials and cutting box.

2 Several yards of bias strips are needed for all of the appliquéd stems. It is easiest to make long bias tubes and cut them to length as needed. Referring to the figures, fold the bias strips for the stems with wrong sides together and stitch 3/16″ from the *folded* edge. Trim the seam allowance close to the stitching and press the seam so that it is hidden underneath the strip, being careful not to stretch the strip. Cut as needed for the stems.

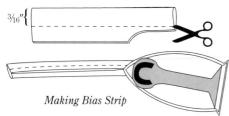

Making Bias Strip

3 When there are many appliquéd blocks that are alike, it is helpful to make a full-size see-through pattern. To make a pattern for the X block, fold an 8½″ square of tracing paper in half vertically. Trace the motif in each half of the paper. To make a pattern for the Y block, fold an 8½″ square of tracing paper in half diagonally, align the fold line with the dotted line of the block Y motif, and trace. Turn the paper over to complete the design.

For the Z block, *cut* an 8½″ square of tracing paper in half diagonally, then *fold* in half. Align the fold line with the dotted line on the pattern and trace the motifs. Turn the paper over and trace the other half.

4 Make templates from the full-size pattern for each patch. There are complete directions in the General Instructions for making templates and cutting patches for hand or machine appliqué. Cut out the fabric patches.

Turn under 3/16″ allowances and baste. Do not turn under those edges that will be covered by other patches. Using your full-size traced patterns as guides, position, pin, and blindstitch the appliqué on A and B background patches. Make 17 X blocks, 14 Y blocks, and 18 Z blocks.

5 For the sashing, look through the T patches you have cut and select two green or teal T's that look pretty with one red, gold, or purple T. Sew them together to make one sash. Make 80 sashes. Press the seam allowances to one side.

Assembling the Quilt Top

6 The blocks in this quilt are set on point. The setting squares and triangles are the cream U, V, and W patches. The blocks and sashes are sewn together in diagonal rows.

Use the assembly diagram as a guide when joining the rows for the twin-size quilt. Carefully join the blocks

Block Size:	Twin-Size	Wall
8½"	Quilt	Quilt
Quilt Size:	67" x 81¼"	38¾" x 38¾"
Quilt Requires:	17 X Blocks	No X Blocks
	14 Y Blocks	4 Y Blocks
	18 Z Blocks	8 Z Blocks

Materials and Cutting:

Cream Solid	**¼ yd.**	**⅛ yd.**
	32 U, 14 V,	5 U, 4 V,
	4 W	4 W
Red Print	**2¼ yds.**	**1 yd.**
2 borders	1¾" x 75¾"	1¾" x 33¼"
2 borders	1¾" x 61½"	1¾" x 33¼"
binding	2½" x 8½ yds.	2½" x 4½ yds.
(For corded edging, see instructions on page 84.)		
Brown Print	**2½ yds.**	**1¼ yds.**
2 borders	4½" x 83¾"	4½" x 41¼"
2 borders	4½" x 69½"	4½" x 41¼"
Lt. Plaid Scraps	**3 yds.**	**¾ yd.**
	31 A, 18 B	4 A, 8 B
Green Scraps	**3¼ yds.**	**⅞ yd.**
bias for stems	¾" x 24½ yds.	¾" x 4¾ yds.
	34 C, 34 D,	64 E, 24 G,
	320 E, 132 G,	72 H, 20 J,
	348 H, 128 J,	12 K, 12 Kr,
	32 K, 32 Kr,	4 L, 4 Lr,
	14 L, 14 Lr,	4 M, 4 Mr,
	14 M, 14 Mr,	4 O, 4 P,
	14 O, 14 P,	8 R, 8 Rr,
	18 R, 18 Rr,	8 S, 32 T
	18 S, 160 T	
Red/Gold Scraps	**2⅛ yds.**	**½ yd.**
	132 F, 128 I,	24 F, 20 I,
	28 N, 18 Q,	8 N, 8 Q,
	18 Qr, 80 T	8 Qr, 16 T
Lining	**5 yds.**	**2½ yds.**
2 panels	36" x 85¼"	21⅞" x 42¾"
Batting	**71" x 85¼"**	**42¾" x 42¾"**

and sashes to make diagonal block rows. Press the seam allowances in one direction. Join the sashes and cream patches to make sash rows. Press the seam allowances in the direction that is opposite to the block rows. Join the rows. Press the seam allowances between rows in one direction.

Adding the Borders

7 Sew the short red borders to the top and bottom of the quilt. Trim ends even with the raw edges of the quilt. Sew the long red borders to the sides. Likewise, sew the brown print borders to the top and bottom, then on the sides of the quilt.

Taking It to the Finish

8 Press the quilt top. Sew the lining panels together. Layer the quilt lining, batting, and quilt top as explained in the General Instructions. Thread- or pin-baste the layers together.

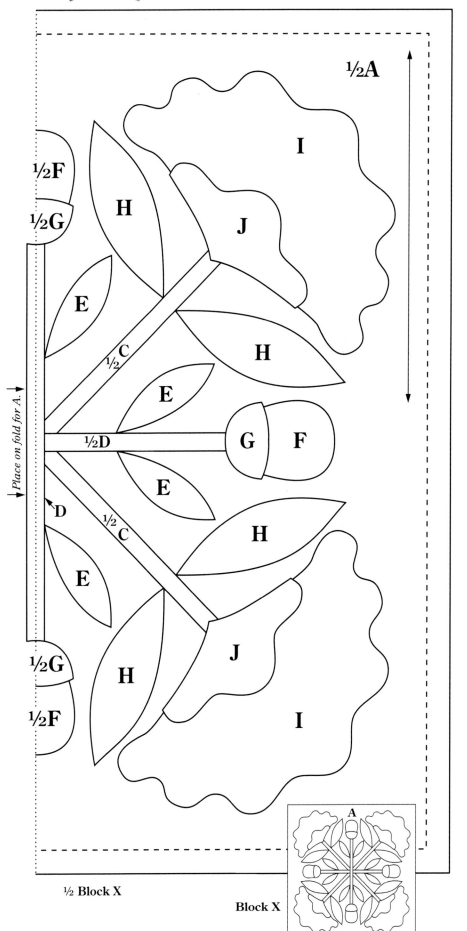

½ Block X

Block X

9 Quilt around all the appliqué patches. Quilt in-the-ditch around the sashes and cream patches. Quilt around some of the flowers or figures in the brown print borders.

10 Read the directions below if you want to make corded edging to finish the quilt as Faye has done, or apply double-fold binding to finish, following the directions in the General Instructions. Remember to sign and date your quilt on the back, perhaps with a special label. Or better yet, embroider your name on the *front* of the quilt in the border, so that everyone can see who the quilt artist is!

WALL QUILT

1 Read Steps 1 through 3 for the twin-size quilt to select fabrics, cut the patches, and prepare the stems and appliqué patches.

2 Look at the block diagrams and the wall quilt assembly diagrams and read Steps 4 and 5 for the twin-size quilt. Then make four Y blocks and eight Z blocks. Make 16 sashes.

3 To help you when sewing the blocks, sashes, and cream patches together to make the quilt top, refer to the wall quilt assembly diagram. Lay out the parts of the quilt in the diagonal rows as shown. **Note:** Be sure to turn the Y blocks so that the flowers meet in the center of the quilt. Join the rows.

4 Read the appropriate steps in the twin-size assembly when you're ready to baste the layers and for quilting your wall quilt.

If desired, add a 3″-wide sleeve on the back of the quilt along the top edge for hanging with a rod, as described in the General Instructions. Don't forget to sign your name on a label on the back of the quilt.

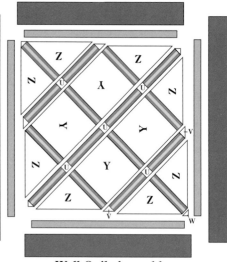

Wall Quilt Assembly

CORDED EDGING

Corded edging adds an elegant finish to the edge of this quilt. The yardage given in the materials and cutting box for binding is sufficient for this method. In addition, you need to purchase 8⅜ yards of ³⁄₁₆″ - ¼″ cording for the twin-size quilt, or 4½ yards of cording for the wall quilt.

From the red print used for the borders, cut 1″-wide bias strips to total 17½ yards for the twin-size quilt or 9½ yards for the wall quilt. Half of this bias stripping will be used to cover the cord and half will be used to stitch the corded edging in place.

The quilt has curved corners so that the edging can be easily stitched in place. Using a bowl or cup as a guide, mark and cut a curve at each corner of the outer border of the quilt.

Stitch ⅛″ from the raw edge all around the quilt through all layers. Trim the batting and lining even with the quilt top.

The bias strips are sewn together end to end at a 45-degree angle (see figure). To prepare the bias strips for

sewing, use a 45-degree line on an acrylic ruler or a 2″ square of paper folded in half diagonally as a guide, and cut the ends of the bias strips at an angle. With right sides together, sew half of the bias strips together end to end. Repeat with the other half. Press the seam allowances open.

To make the corded edging, place the purchased cording on the wrong side of the bias strip. Fold the bias over the cording, aligning the raw edges of the bias strip. Using a zipper foot and thread to match the bias strip, stitch close to the cording (see figure).

Position the corded edging on top of the quilt with all raw edges aligned; ease the cording around the corners. Overlap the ends of the corded edging where they meet (see figure). Stitch on top of the previous row of stitching near the cording.

With right sides together and raw

Cording being stitched into bias strip

Overlapping ends of corded edging

edges aligned, place the remaining 1″-wide bias strip on top of the quilt so that the corded edging is caught in between the layers (see figure). Again, using the zipper foot, stitch through all layers close to the cording. Turn under and overlap the ends where they meet.

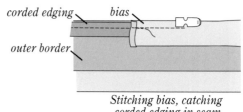

Stitching bias, catching corded edging in seam

Turn under ¼″ along the raw edge of the 1″ bias strip. Turn the bias strip to the back side of the quilt and blindstitch the folded edge to the lining. The corded edging now forms the edge of the quilt. Make small pleats at the corners as needed.

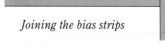

Joining the bias strips

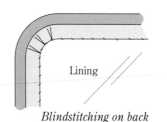

Blindstitching on back

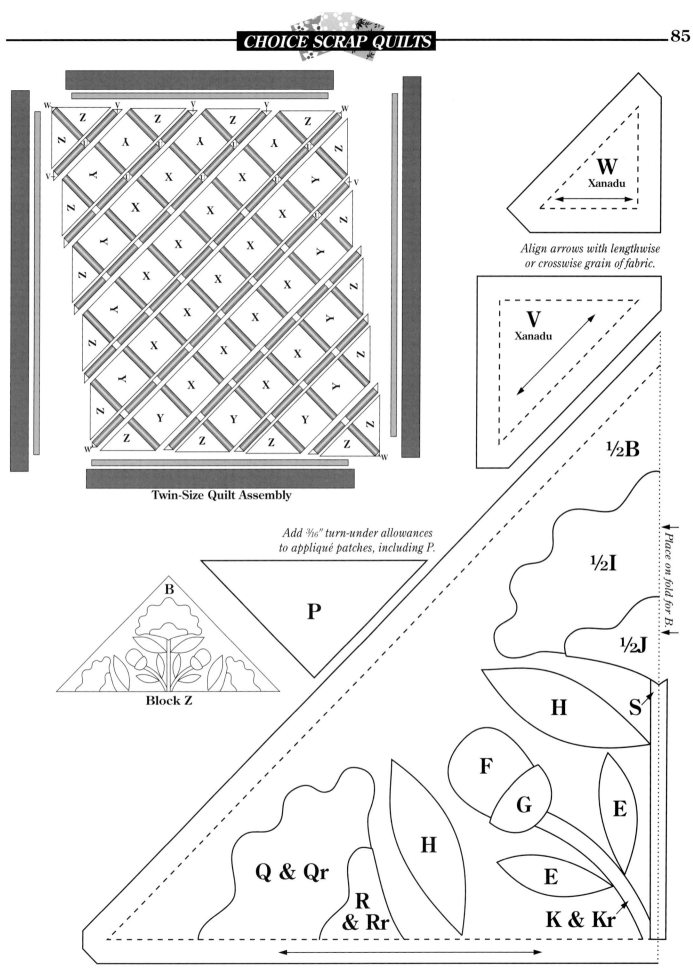

Twin-Size Quilt Assembly

W
Xanadu

Align arrows with lengthwise or crosswise grain of fabric.

V
Xanadu

½**B**

½**I**

½**J**

Place on fold for B.

S

H

½ **Block Z**

Add ³⁄₁₆" turn-under allowances to appliqué patches, including P.

B

P

Block Z

H

F

G

E

E

Q & Qr

R & Rr

K & Kr

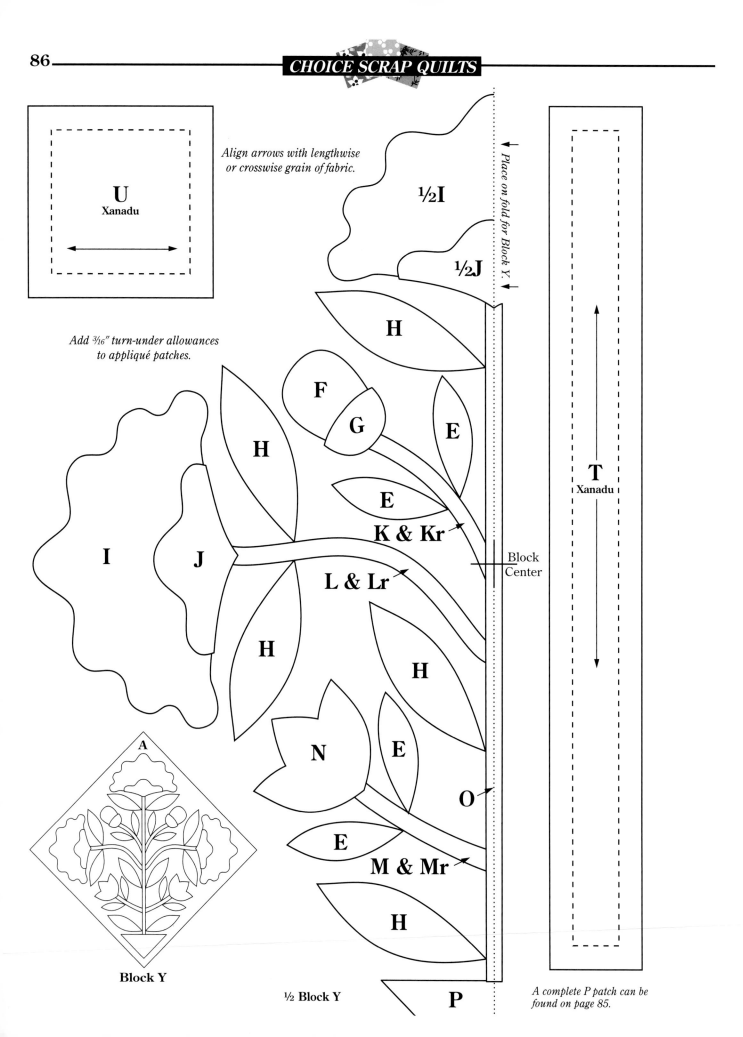

U
Xanadu

Align arrows with lengthwise
or crosswise grain of fabric.

Add ³⁄₁₆" turn-under allowances
to appliqué patches.

½I

½J

Place on fold for Block Y.

H

F

G

E

H

E

E

K & Kr

Block
Center

L & Lr

I

J

H

H

N

E

O

E

M & Mr

H

T
Xanadu

A

Block Y

½ Block Y

P

*A complete P patch can be
found on page 85.*

Stephanie's Scrap Garden

Designed and made by Stephanie Martin Glennon

A romantic garden of flowers awaits you in this radiant quilt! In it, jewel-toned flowers are set in frames of various shades of green, and all are interspersed in a galaxy of eight-pointed stars. The star-like flowers in the border are appliquéd in place along with their delicate stems and simple leaves. Every color of the rainbow has been used for the flowers. Each flower is made of four different fabrics, all in the same color family, surrounded by a whorl of "leaves" in four different shades of green.

To simplify your choices, you can organize your fabrics into color families of pinks, blues, greens, etc. Then, within each family, separate the fabrics into lights, mediums, and darks. This process is fun and easy to do, and it will allow you to see at a glance which fabrics will work best for your flowers and which colors may need to be filled in with purchased fabrics.

The wall quilt is made with four of the large blocks, surrounded by the eight-pointed stars. We have left the corners at an angle to give the quilt a contemporary flavor.

FULL-SIZE QUILT

Making the Blocks

1 After you have chosen fabrics for each block, the materials and cutting box will show you how many patches to cut and will give dimensions for borders, binding, lining, and batting. To make it easier to visualize how the blocks are sewn, they have been divided into simple-to-sew units, as shown in the block assembly diagram. Each block has four unit 1's, four unit 2's, and one A patch.

For the quilt to go together quickly and easily, it is important that all blocks be the same size. You may want to make one whole block and measure it. Then, as you make the other blocks, you can check each one for size with the first. It will also be helpful if you draw seam lines on the wrong sides of the diamond patches. That way, you can put a pin through the cross seams to aid in matching them. Make 16 flower blocks for the full-size quilt.

Assembling the Quilt Top

2 Now it's time to put the F framing strips on each block. In Stephanie's quilt, all framing strips around a block are cut from the same fabric, which helps to unify the quilt. Notice that the blocks alternate subtly between light and dark in a checkerboard fashion. The flowers are a little lighter or brighter in the light blocks, and the green framing strips are also lighter. Stitch an F framing strip on each side of each block.

The star units, which are sewn on last, are made by joining one light/medium I, one medium Ir, one cream J, and two cream H's. (The I and Ir patches are in the same color family.) You will need to make four identical star units in nine color combinations, with a different color family for each eight-pointed star, for a total of 36 units. On a large flat surface, lay out all the framed blocks in the or-

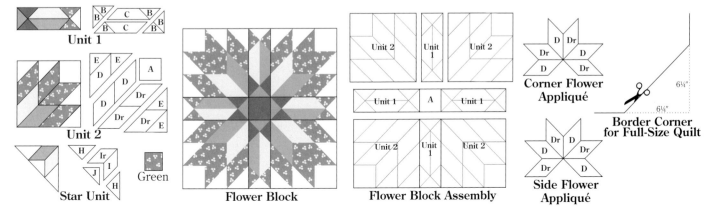

Unit 1

Unit 2

Star Unit

Green

Flower Block

Flower Block Assembly

Corner Flower Appliqué

Border Corner for Full-Size Quilt

Side Flower Appliqué

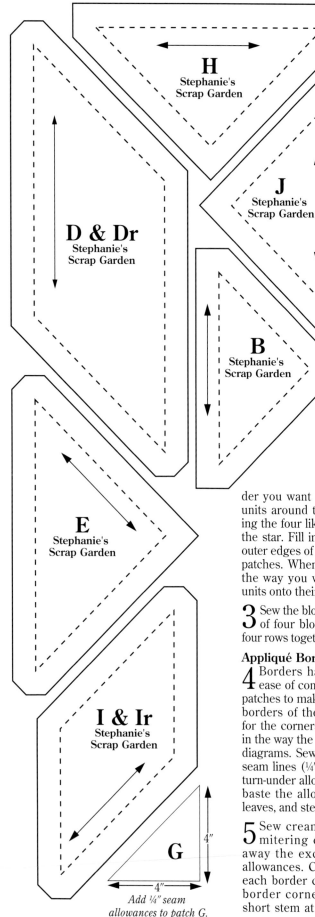

H
Stephanie's
Scrap Garden

J
Stephanie's
Scrap Garden

D & Dr
Stephanie's
Scrap Garden

B
Stephanie's
Scrap Garden

E
Stephanie's
Scrap Garden

I & Ir
Stephanie's
Scrap Garden

G

*Add ¼″ seam
allowances to patch G.*

Block Size: 14″	Full-Size Quilt	Wall Quilt
Quilt Size:	88″ x 88″	50″ x 50″
Quilt Requires:	16 Blocks	4 Blocks
	36 Star Units	36 Star Units
	4 Corner Flowers	
	12 Side Flowers	

Materials and Cutting:

	Full-Size Quilt	Wall Quilt
Cream 4 borders	4¼ yds.	1⅝ yds.
	8½″ x 90½″	16 A, 16 B, 64 E,
	64 A, 64 B, 256 E,	72 H, 36 J, 8 M,
	28 G, 72 H, 36 J	4 N, 4 O
Green Scraps	4 yds.	1½ yds.
	128 B, 128 D, 128 Dr,	32 B, 32 D, 32 Dr,
	64 F, 24 K, 8 L	24 F
	12 stems ¾″ x 8″	
	4 stems ¾″ x 6″	
Solid and Print Scraps	3⅛ yds.	1 yd.
	16 A, 192 B, 128 C,	4 A, 48 B, 32 C,
	112 D, 112 Dr, 36 I,	16 D, 16 Dr, 36 I,
	36 Ir	36 Ir
Binding	⅞ yd.	½ yd.
	2½″ x 10⅝ yds.	2½″ x 6⅓ yds.
Lining 3 panels	8 yds.	3¼ yds.
2 panels	31″ x 92″	27¼″ x 54″
Batting	92″ x 92″	54″ x 54″

der you want them. Place all the star units around the center blocks, keeping the four like units together to form the star. Fill in the corners around the outer edges of the blocks with cream G patches. When everything is arranged the way you want it, sew all the star units onto their respective blocks.

3 Sew the blocks together in four rows of four blocks each. Then sew the four rows together.

Appliqué Borders

4 Borders have been simplified for ease of construction. Join D and Dr patches to make 12 flowers for the side borders of the quilt and four flowers for the corners, noting the differences in the way the patches are joined in the diagrams. Sew only to the ends of the seam lines (¼″ from the raw edge) for turn-under allowances. Turn under and baste the allowances of the flowers, leaves, and stems.

5 Sew cream borders to quilt top, mitering corners and trimming away the excess to leave ¼″ seam allowances. Cut off a 6¼″ triangle at each border corner, as shown in the border corner diagram. Position a short stem at the edge of the corner

cream G patch as shown here. Pin it diagonally across G and onto the mitered corner of the outer border. Likewise, fold under one end of a long stem and position it over the seam of the two cream G's where two blocks meet, and extend it into the outer border. Position side and corner flowers, keeping outer points at least ¼″ inside cut edge of border to allow for the binding, then position the leaves. Appliqué patches in place using the blind stitch or your favorite stitch. Press the quilt top.

Taking It to the Finish

6 Sew the lining panels together. Layer quilt lining, batting, and top, and then baste the quilt sandwich, either with thread or with safety pins. Decide on a quilting plan. As a suggestion, you can outline quilt the pieced

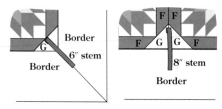

Positioning Stems

patches ¼″ from seams and quilt in-the-ditch around the appliquéd patches. Using strips of masking tape placed on the quilt top as a guide, you can quilt the border in diagonal parallel straight lines approximately 1″ apart. Apply double-fold binding, pleating to ease it at the angled corners. Don't forget to add a label.

WALL QUILT

1 Follow instructions in Steps 1 and 2 for the full-size quilt, except you need only four flower blocks. You still need the 36 star units in nine color combinations, for the nine eight-pointed stars at the corners of the blocks.

2 Study the wall quilt assembly diagram as you arrange the framed blocks in two rows of two. Add the star units, keeping like colors together. Sew blocks together. An outer border unit is made with a green F, a cream M, and two star units. Make eight of these. Following the assembly diagram, sew the pieced border units and the extra star units at the ends of the top and bottom pieced borders to the quilt.

3 Sew the four cream N's to the quilt and add the O patches.

4 Follow Step 6 of the full-size assembly to complete the wall quilt. Make one long continuous straight-grain binding strip, begin along one side of the quilt, and pleat the binding to ease it at the angled corners. If desired, add a 3″-wide sleeve on the back of the quilt along the top edge for hanging with a rod.

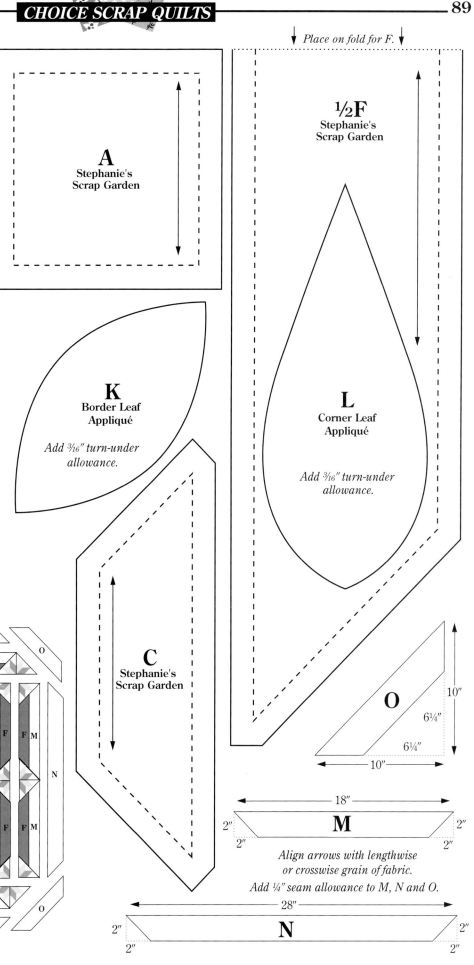

Place on fold for F.

½F
Stephanie's Scrap Garden

A
Stephanie's Scrap Garden

K
Border Leaf Appliqué

Add ³⁄₁₆″ turn-under allowance.

L
Corner Leaf Appliqué

Add ³⁄₁₆″ turn-under allowance.

C
Stephanie's Scrap Garden

O

10″
6¼″
6¼″
10″

M
18″
2″
2″
2″
2″

Align arrows with lengthwise or crosswise grain of fabric.

Add ¼″ seam allowance to M, N and O.

N
28″
2″
2″
2″
2″

Wall Quilt Assembly

Tulips and Butterflies

Designed and made by Yoshiko Taniuchi

The perky, springtime colors in this design are sure to lift your spirits as you stitch it, and the finished quilt will give a smile and a better day to all who see it. It is an ideal pattern for clear, bright scraps.

We offer directions for two sizes, one of them perfect for a wall quilt or child's quilt, or as a charming conversation piece centered over a spread on a double or larger bed. The other size is an unusual display piece to go above a headboard, couch, or mantle. It also would make a festive table runner for a spring or summer party.

The design is comprised of three blocks: a butterfly block, tulip block, and leaf block. Each of them is so easy to make that any beginning quiltmaker should feel no hesitancy about choosing this pattern. The tulip block has one set-in seam, but for first-time quiltmakers, easy-to-follow directions are given for this technique in the General Instructions.

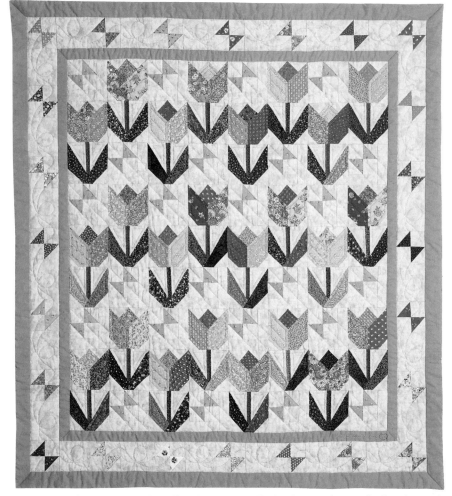

WALL / CHILD'S QUILT

Making the Blocks

1 Choose a light blue print with a small, busy print, or a mottled "sky" print. The print will help hide the seams in the butterfly blocks. Sort and prepare fabrics for cutting. You will find recommendations for fabric preparation in the chapter on Working With Scraps.

2 Cut patches as listed in the box. Referring to block piecing diagrams, join patches A, Ar, B, C, and D to make 24 tulip blocks. Make 24 butterfly blocks with patches E, F, G, and H. Join patches F, I, J, Jr, K, and L to make 24 leaf blocks.

3 Referring to the row 1 diagram, join three of each type of block in a verti-cal row. Make four row 1's. Likewise, make four row 2's. Join rows, referring to the wall quilt assembly diagram.

Adding the Borders

4 Sew the long 1½″ borders to the sides of the finished section; sew the short 1½″ borders to the top and bottom edges. Miter the corners and trim the excess fabric to leave ¼″ seam allowances.

5 Referring to butterfly border unit piecing diagram, make 24 butterfly units. Notice that these butterflies "fly" in the opposite direction from those in the blocks. It may be helpful to lay out the butterfly units on a table to check orientation.

6 To make a side border, join six N's and five butterfly units alternately, being careful to sew the butterflies to the short edges of N's. Again, we suggest you lay them out in order before sewing, just to make sure the orientation is correct. Sew border to side of quilt top. Repeat for the other side.

7 To make the top border, join seven butterfly units alternately with six M patches, being careful to sew the butterflies to the short edges of M's. Sew border to top of quilt. Repeat for the bottom border. Sew the 2″ borders to the quilt, mitering corners and trimming excess. Press the quilt top.

Taking It to the Finish

8 Mark quilting design in the M and N patches. Sew the lining panels together. Assemble and baste the lining, batting, and quilt top.

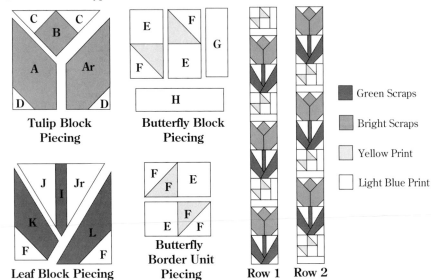

Tulip Block Piecing

Butterfly Block Piecing

Leaf Block Piecing

Butterfly Border Unit Piecing

Row 1   **Row 2**

■ Green Scraps

■ Bright Scraps

□ Yellow Print

□ Light Blue Print

9 Outline quilt tulip, leaf, and stem patches ¼″ from seams. As shown in photo, quilt diagonal lines across butterfly blocks. Quilt marked lines in M and N patches, and continue those curving lines across adjacent butterfly units. Quilt in-the-ditch next to the medium blue borders.

10 Finish the edges of the quilt with your favorite method or by turning in ¼″ seam allowances on quilt top and lining. Blindstitch the edge. (See the directions on this page.)

TABLE RUNNER

1 Follow instructions for the 43″ x 47″ quilt, except make nine each of the tulip, leaf, and butterfly blocks.

2 Arrange blocks as shown in the table runner assembly diagram. Working one row a time, join blocks in vertical rows. Join rows.

3 Sew the short borders to the sides of the quilt top; sew the long borders to the top and bottom edges of the quilt top. Miter the corners and trim the excess to leave ¼″ seam allowances. Press the quilt top.

4 Sew the lining panels together. Assemble and baste the lining, batting, and quilt top.

5 Outline quilt tulip, leaf, and stem patches ¼″ from seams. As shown in photo of the larger version, quilt diagonal lines across butterfly blocks. Quilt in-the-ditch next to the medium blue borders.

6 Finish the edges of the quilt by turning in ¼″ seam allowances on quilt top and lining. Blindstitch the edge.

Block Size: 4″	Wall/Child's Quilt	Table Runner
Quilt Size:	43″ x 47″	39″ x 15″
Quilt Requires:	24 Tulip Blocks	9 Tulip Blocks
	24 Butterfly Blocks	9 Butterfly Blocks
	24 Leaf Blocks	9 Leaf Blocks
Materials and Cutting:		
Lt. Blue Print	1¾ yds.	⅝ yd.
	48 C, 48 D, 96 E,	18 C, 18 D, 18 E,
	144 F, 24 G, 24 H,	36 F, 9 G, 9 H,
	24 J, 24 Jr, 12 M,	9 J, 9 Jr
	12 N	
Med. Blue Solid	1½ yds.*	1⅜ yds.*
2 borders	2″ x 47½″	2″ x 39½″
2 borders	2″ x 43½″	2″ x 15½″
2 borders	1½″ x 38½″	(No 1½″ borders)
2 borders	1½″ x 34½″	
Yellow Print	¼ yd.	⅛ yd.
	48 F	18 F
Green Scraps	¾ yd.	⅜ yd.
	24 I, 24 K, 24 L	9 I, 9 K, 9 L
Bright Scraps	⅞ yd.	⅜ yd.
	24 A, 24 Ar,	9 A, 9 Ar, 9 B
	24 B, 48 F	
Lining	2⅞ yds.*	1⅜ yds.*
2 panels	26″ x 47″	
1 panel		43″ x 19″
Batting	47″ x 51″	43″ x 19″

Border measurements are the exact length needed plus seam allowances.

*NOTE: For the wall quilt, if you purchase 2⅞ yards of medium blue solid, you will have enough fabric to cut out all the borders and the lining panels. For the table runner, 1⅜ yards will provide both the borders and the lining if you want the borders and lining to be cut from the same fabric.

NOTE: There is no binding on these quilts.

FINISHING THE QUILT EDGES WITHOUT BINDING

Binding is the most-used method for finishing the edges of a quilt, but there is another technique that is very easy to do. The seam allowances on the quilt top and lining can simply be turned to the inside and sewn by hand for a smooth finish. The edges of the quilt will be most attractive if you use the same fabric for both the outer border and the lining.

This technique is best for quilts that will not get hard use. A baby quilt, for example, will wear longer if the edges are bound. Another point to consider is that binding will hold the batting in place better than this method will. Still, this technique is worth a try for an easy

finish on a wall quilt. And because pressing and machine sewing are not required, with this method you can complete your quilt away from home.

Prepare for this no-binding finish by quilting or tying all but the outer ½″ of the quilt. Do not quilt the outer ½″ now, but remember that the quilting can be completed after the edges are finished if your quilting design includes that area.

Stabilize the edges of the quilt with

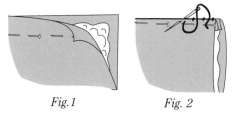

Fig. 1   *Fig. 2*

pins every few inches (see Fig. 1). Trim the batting to be ¼″ smaller than the quilt top. The trimmed size will be the finished size of the quilt. Trim the lining to match the quilt top.

Turn under edges of the lining ¼″ and fold them over the batting. Use your fingers to press a soft crease. Turn under the edges of the quilt top ¼″ and use pins to hold the layers together. All raw edges are turned to the inside.

Using a single strand of thread that matches the border fabric on the quilt top, sew the folded edges with a blind stitch (see Fig. 2). Remove the pins as you sew.

Finish the quilting around the edges if necessary. A line of machine quilting ¼″ from the edge is a nice touch and will secure the batting.

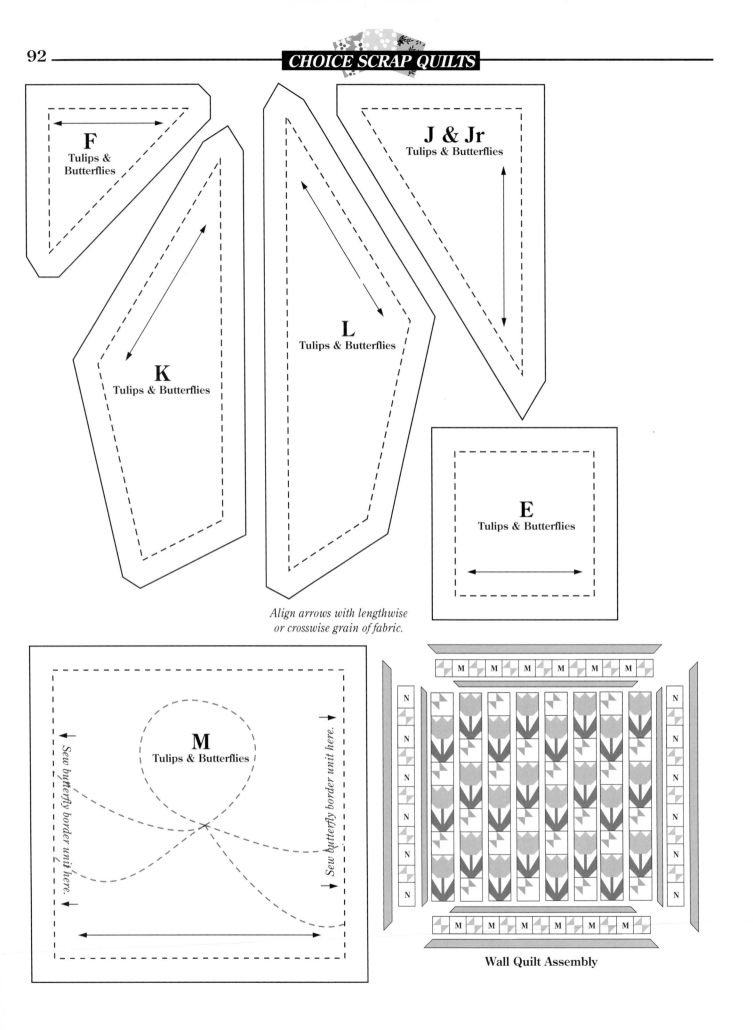

F
Tulips & Butterflies

K
Tulips & Butterflies

L
Tulips & Butterflies

J & Jr
Tulips & Butterflies

E
Tulips & Butterflies

Align arrows with lengthwise or crosswise grain of fabric.

M
Tulips & Butterflies

Sew butterfly border unit here.

Sew butterfly border unit here.

Wall Quilt Assembly

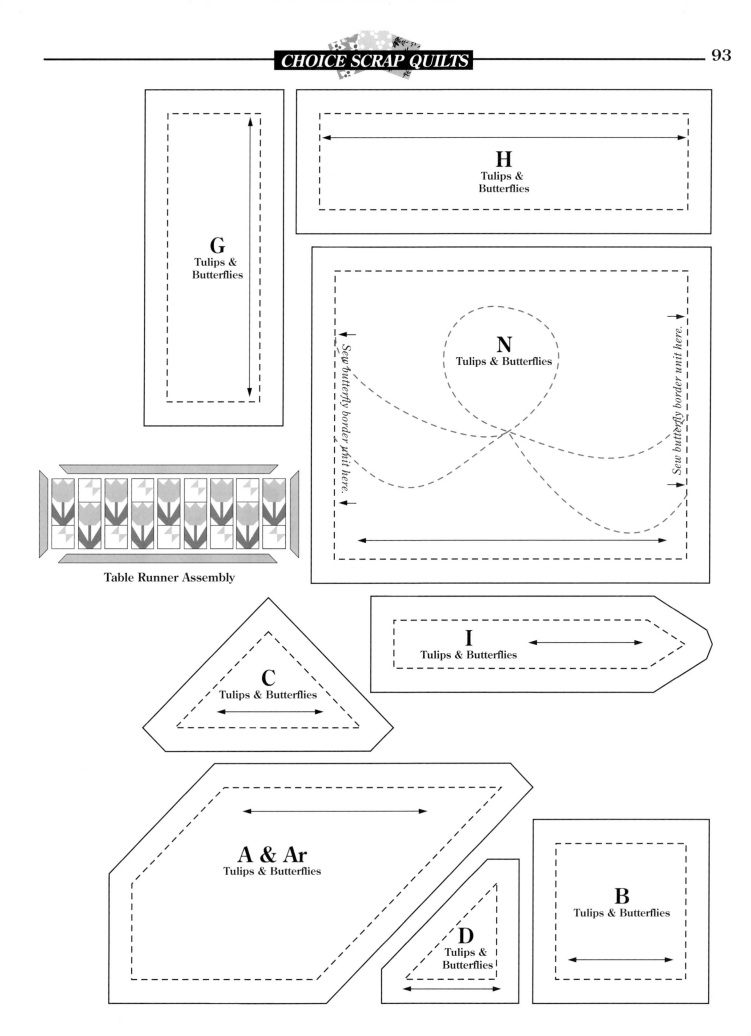

G
Tulips &
Butterflies

H
Tulips &
Butterflies

N
Tulips & Butterflies

Sew butterfly border unit here.

Sew butterfly border unit here.

Table Runner Assembly

I
Tulips & Butterflies

C
Tulips & Butterflies

A & Ar
Tulips & Butterflies

D
Tulips &
Butterflies

B
Tulips & Butterflies

Circle of Friends

Designed by Judy Martin, made by Jenny Hubbard and Maria Reardon Capp

Tradition combines with a timesaving way of piecing this design, which is a twist on the favorite Double Wedding Ring. We've eliminated the curves to simplify the piecing, but the illusion of interlocking rings remains. If you've pieced even one quilt before, this charming full-size quilt will be easy to make, and the wall quilt will take even less time. Color choice and placement are simple—just use light and dark versions of four different colorways. With its cheerful circles bursting into stars where they touch, this quilt celebrates the joys of friendship. Wouldn't it make a lovely friendship presentation from your circle of friends to one you care for? We've tied this quilt with the invisible tying method described in the General Instructions, but we've also included quilting suggestions in the assembly text.

FULL-SIZE QUILT

Sewing and Arranging Blocks

1 Gather your favorite scraps, perhaps ones that you and your quilting friends have exchanged with each other. Sort them into lights and darks for each of four color groups. For this quilt we chose light and dark gold, light and dark blue, light and dark pink, and light and dark green, along with two shades of yellow for the stars. We used a single fabric for the cream background.

Cut patches as listed in the materials and cutting box. The drawings for block Y and block Z show how the patches go together in each of the two block colorations. On a table, lay out the patches as in the block drawings, being sure to put the light and dark patches in the right places to keep the effect of interlocking circles. Make one

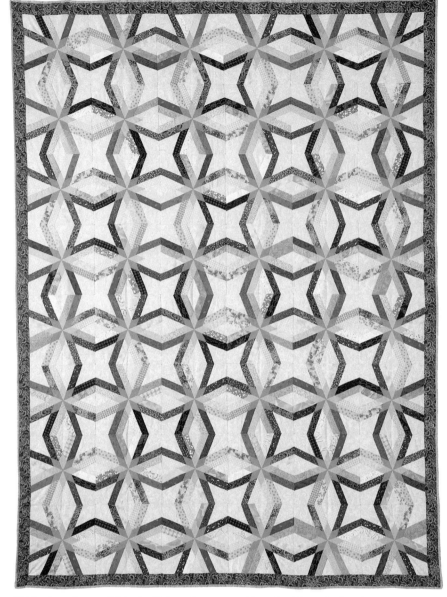

Y block and one Z block. Using them as guides, make a total of 24 Y blocks and 24 Z blocks.

2 Look at the top row of blocks in the quilt photo. You'll see that the effect

of interlocking circles does not appear until the blocks are joined into rows. For the first row, join three Y blocks alternately with three Z blocks. Start with a Y block on the far left end, and be sure to turn the block so that the green

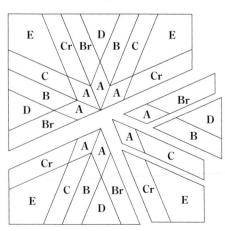

Blocks Y & Z Piecing

★ **Light Yellow** ● **Dark Yellow**

Block Y

Block Z

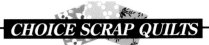

Block Size: 12″	Full-Size Quilt	Wall Quilt
Quilt Size:	76″ x 100″	52″ x 52″
Quilt Requires:	24 Y blocks 24 Z blocks	8 Y blocks 8 Z blocks
Materials and Cutting:		
Cream Solid	**3¼ yds.** 192 D, 192 E	**1¼ yds.** 64 D, 64 E
Lt. Yellow Solid	**⅞ yd.** 192 A	**⅜ yd.** 64 A
Dk. Yellow Solid	**⅞ yd.** 192 A	**⅜ yd.** 64 A
Lt. Gold Scraps	**⅞ yd.** 48 B, 48 Br	**⅜ yd.** 16 B, 16 Br
Dk. Gold Scraps	**⅞ yd.** 48 C, 48 Cr	**⅜ yd.** 16 C, 16 Cr
Lt. Green Scraps	**⅞ yd.** 48 B, 48 Br	**⅜ yd.** 16 B, 16 Br
Dk. Green Scraps	**⅞ yd.** 48 C, 48 Cr	**⅜ yd.** 16 C, 16 Cr
Lt. Pink Scraps	**⅞ yd.** 48 B, 48 Br	**⅜ yd.** 16 B, 16 Br
Dk. Pink Scraps	**⅞ yd.** 48 C, 48 Cr	**⅜ yd.** 16 C, 16 Cr
Lt. Blue Scraps binding	**1¾ yds.** 2½″ x 10⅝ yds. 48 B, 48 Br	**⅞ yd.** 2½″ x 6⅜ yds 16 B, 16 Br
Dk. Blue Print 2 borders 2 borders	**3 yds.** 2½″ x 102½″ 2½″ x 78½″ 48 C, 48 Cr	**1¾ yds.** 2½″ x 54½″ 2½″ x 54½″ 16 C, 16 Cr
Lining 3 panels 2 panels	**6⅛ yds.** 35¼″ x 80″	**3⅜ yds.** 28½″ x 56″
Batting	**80″ x 104″**	**56″ x 56″**

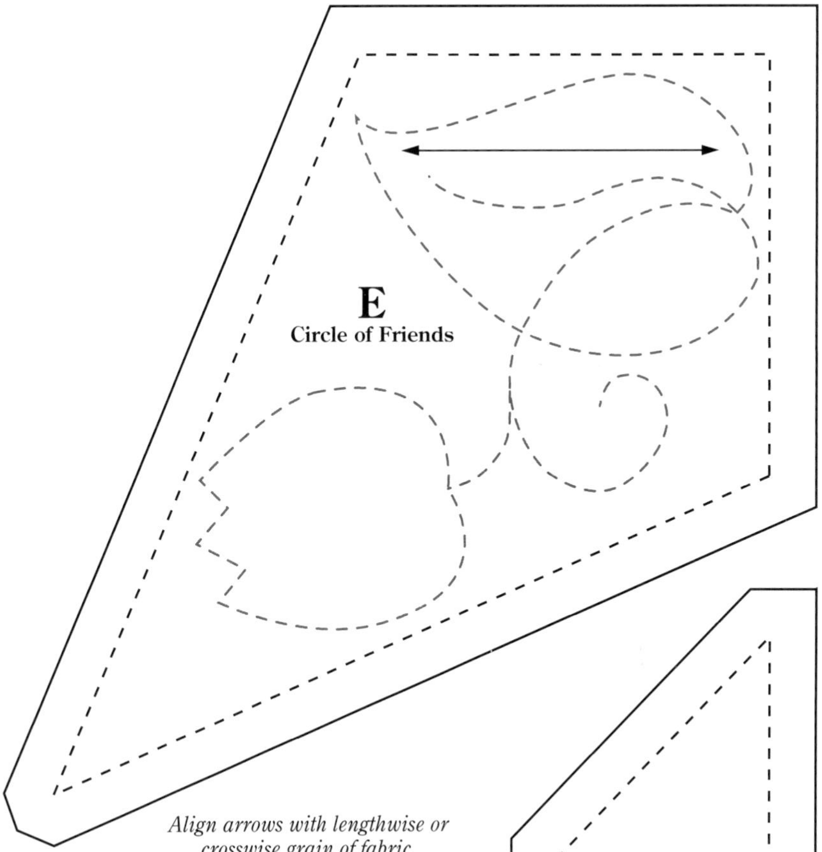
E
Circle of Friends

Align arrows with lengthwise or crosswise grain of fabric.

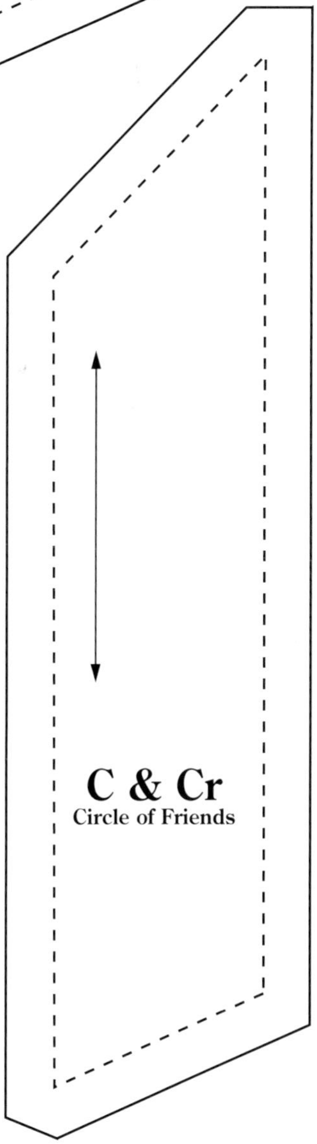
C & Cr
Circle of Friends

and gold patches are at the top of the block, like the block in the uppermost left corner of the quilt. As you join the blocks, be careful to rotate the blocks so that the rings of color match where they touch–for instance, the light and dark gold patches at the edge of a block Y should touch the light and dark gold patches at the edge of a block Z. After you've completed the first row, check it against the quilt photo to be sure the color placement is right. Then make eight rows like this.

Assembling the Quilt Top

3 Join the rows, turning alternate rows upside down so that you can see the formation of the interlocking color rings. Be sure that a Y block is on the far left end of odd-numbered rows, a Z block is on the far left end of even-numbered rows, and Y blocks touch Z blocks.

4 Fold each border strip to find the center. Then fold the quilt top in half both ways to find the center of each side. Matching centers, sew short borders to the top and bottom of the quilt top, stopping stitching ¼″ from the quilt edge. Sew long borders to the sides. Miter corners, trimming excess from seam allowances.

Taking It to the Finish

5 Press the quilt top. Mark the quilting motifs in the E patches if you plan to hand or machine quilt. Sew the lining panels together, then layer the quilt lining, batting, and top as explained in the General Instructions. Pin or thread-baste the layers together.

6 Quilt motifs in E patches. We suggest outline quilting all other patches to help emphasize the interlocking-ring effect. Quilt the borders in-the-ditch. When you have finished your quilting, apply double-fold binding in a light blue print, as described in the General Instructions. We have given a diagram on the next page for tying the quilt if you choose that option.

Don't forget to sign and date your quilt on the back!

WALL QUILT

1 Follow the instructions given in Step 1 of the full-size assembly but make only eight Y blocks and eight Z blocks.

2 The instructions given in Step 2 of the full-size assembly apply here as well, but you should have only four blocks in each row. Check your color placement as you go, and sew two Y blocks alternately with two Z blocks. Be careful to turn all blocks exactly as they appear in the block diagrams. A Y block should be on the far left end.

Make four rows like this.

3 Join the rows, turning alternate rows upside down so that you can see the formation of the interlocking color rings. A Y block should be on the far left end of odd-numbered rows, a Z block should be on the far left end of even-numbered rows, and Y blocks should touch Z blocks.

4 Fold border strips and the quilt top to find centers as described in Step 4 of the full-size assembly. Sew a dark blue border strip to each edge of the quilt top, matching centers, and stop-ping stitching ¼" from quilt edge. Miter corners, trimming excess from seam allowances.

5 Press the quilt top, then mark the quilting motifs in the E patches if you plan to hand or machine quilt. Sew the lining panels together, then layer the quilt lining, batting, and top as explained in the General Instructions. Pin or thread-baste the layers together.

6 See Step 6 in the full-size quilt instructions to finish. If desired, add a 3"-wide sleeve along the top back edge of the quilt for hanging with a rod.

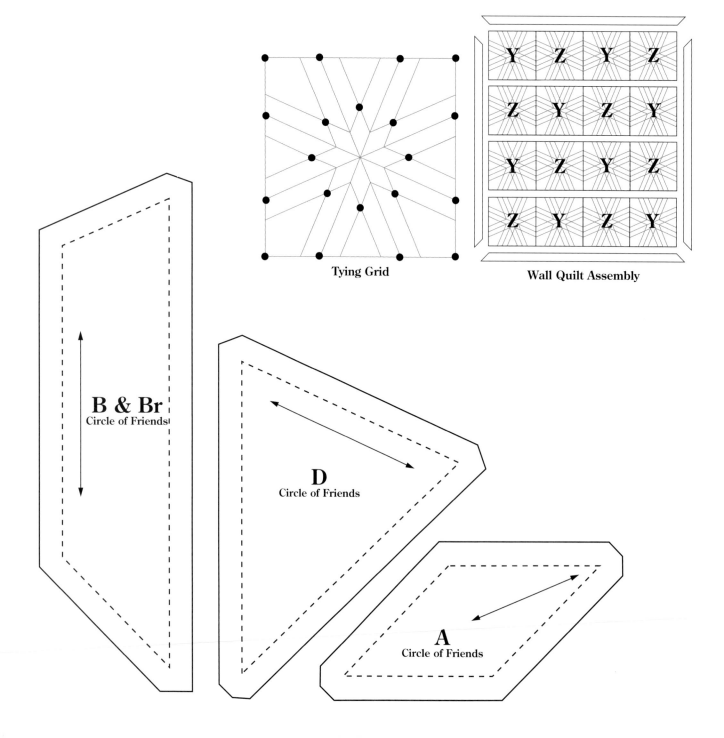

Tying Grid

Wall Quilt Assembly

B & Br
Circle of Friends

D
Circle of Friends

A
Circle of Friends

Coming Up Sunshine

Designed and made by Marion L. Huyck

Scraps take on an elegant air in this wonderful wall quilt. Some of the rays of the sun are light on a dark background, and some are the reverse, which gives a flickering movement to the pattern. The designer used the traditional Crown of Thorns block and added her own special touches with an appliqué border and a tree in each corner. It was shown on the cover of Quilter's Newsletter Magazine *issue No. 196 in October 1987.*

The curved section of small triangles in the Sunshine block and the star-shaped appliqué patches in the border will be challenging, but the results will be worth the effort. We give you suggestions for two easy ways to be accurate with the triangles. You can make this design in two sizes, the original wall quilt with nine blocks or a full-size quilt with 20 blocks.

When you begin to select fabrics for this pattern, notice that four units are used in each Sunshine block. In each unit, all of the C patches are cut from one fabric and the D, E, and Er patches are cut from another fabric. Of course, you may want to color the units differently. A dark fabric for the sashes and inner border gives a grid effect, and a light, soft print for the outer border frames the center well. The appliquéd vine adds a touch of folk-art charm.

WALL QUILT

Making the Sunshine Blocks

1 Make templates, following the directions for either machine or hand piecing given in the General Instructions. Cut out patches and mark dots on the curved edges on the wrong side of fabric. To make a Sunshine unit, begin with the arc of C, D, E, and Er patches. Stitch the A and B patches together, then add them to the pieced arc. Stitch the F and Fr patches together, then stitch them to the completed section. Make 36 units.

2 Arrange four Sunshine units, four dark blue G's, and a red H in rows as shown in the block piecing diagram, rotating the units to form the design. Join units and patches in rows, then join rows.

3 Join Sunshine blocks in three rows of three blocks. Pin carefully before stitching to make sure the seams of the sashing meet accurately. Join the rows together in the same way.

Making the Borders

4 Join pastel floral and green patches in rows as shown in the Tree block piecing diagram. Stitch rows together. Add N patches to two sides. Make four

Tree blocks for corners. Set these blocks aside until the rest of the border is completed.

5 Prepare the vines for the long borders by sewing 2"-wide bias strips end to end to make a strip 56" long. Fold strip in half lengthwise with wrong sides together as shown in the figure below. Make a line of stitching

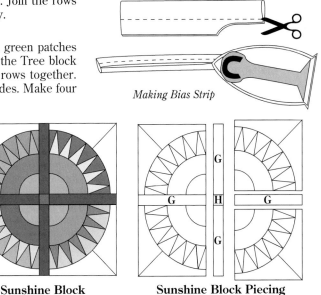

Making Bias Strip

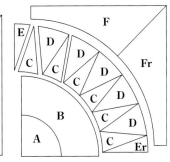
Sunshine Unit   **Sunshine Unit Piecing**

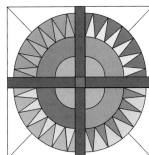
Sunshine Block

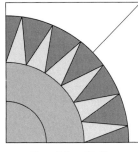
Sunshine Block Piecing

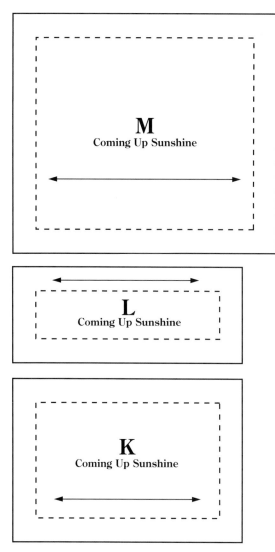

Block Sizes:	Wall Quilt	Full-Size Quilt
Sunshine Block: 14½″	9	20
Tree Block: 7¾″	4	4
Quilt Size:	65″ x 65″	79½″ x 94″

Materials and Cutting:

Pastel Floral Print	2⅛ yds.	3 yds.
2 borders	8¼″ x 46¾″	8¼″ x 75¾″
2 borders	8¼″ x 46¾″	8¼″ x 61¼″
bias binding	1½″ x 7½ yds.	1½″ x 10½ yds.
	16 I, 32 J, 8 K,	16 I, 32 J, 8 K,
	4 M, 8 N, 8 O	4 M, 8 N, 8 O
Dk. Blue Print	1⅜ yds.	2¼ yds.
2 borders	1⅞″ x 46¾″	1⅞″ x 75¾″
2 borders	1⅞″ x 44″	1⅞″ x 58½″
	36 G	80 G
Dk. Green 1	½ yd.	⅝ yd.
	32 I, 8 L, 32 P	32 I, 8 L, 40 P
Dk. Green 2	⅝ yd.	¾ yd.
2 bias strips	2″ x 56″	2″ x 90″
2 bias strips	2″ x 56″	2″ x 70″
stems	12 1″ x 2½″	16 1″ x 2½″
Bright Scraps	3⅜ yds.	7⅛ yds.
	36 A, 36 B,	80 A, 80 B,
	216 C, 180 D,	480 C, 400 D,
	36 E, 36 Er,	80 E, 80 Er,
	36 F, 36 Fr,	80 F, 80 Fr,
	8 R, 8 S	10 R, 10 S
Red Scraps	¼ yd.	¼ yd.
	9 H, 12 Q	20 H, 14 Q
Lining	4 yds.	7⅜ yds.
2 panels	35″ x 69″	
3 panels		33″ x 83½″
Batting	69″ x 69″	83½″ x 98″

½″ from the *folded* edge. Trim the excess seam allowance close to the stitching. Press the strip with the seam underneath. Make four vines.

Prepare the stems by folding the 1″-wide bias strips in half lengthwise with wrong sides together. Make a line of stitching ¼″ from *folded* edge. Finish as for vines. Make 12 stems.

6 Turn under ³⁄₁₆″ allowance on all appliqué patches and baste. It is not necessary to turn under edges of patches that will be tucked under other appliqués. Clip into the corners of the small stars if needed, as in figure.

Clipping the inner corners

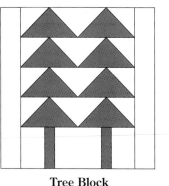

Tree Block

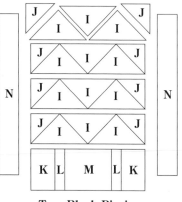

Tree Block Piecing

7 Fold an 8¼″-wide pastel border in half crosswise and finger crease the center. Fold again to divide border in fourths. Mark the center of a long bias vine strip. Place the strip on the border, matching centers. Vine should begin about 3″ from the end of the border strip.

Referring to quilt photo, arrange the vine so that the curves are evenly spaced along the border. The curves of the vine should come within about 1½″ of the raw edge of the border. Baste the vine in place. Arrange stems, leaves, and flowers as shown, and baste. Blind-stitch appliqué patches, using small close stitches and matching thread. Be sure to stitch very closely on the inner corners of the small stars so that the edges don't ravel. Use this method to make all four borders.

Adding the Borders to the Quilt

8 Sew short dark blue borders to the top and bottom of the quilt. Sew long dark blue borders to sides.

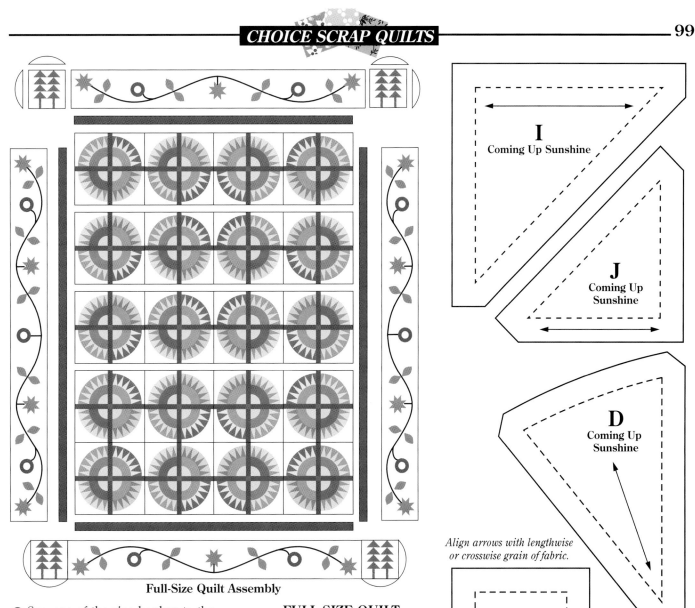

Full-Size Quilt Assembly

I Coming Up Sunshine

J Coming Up Sunshine

D Coming Up Sunshine

Align arrows with lengthwise or crosswise grain of fabric.

H Coming Up Sunshine

9 Sew one of the vine borders to the top of the quilt. Repeat for the bottom. Sew a Tree block to each end of the remaining vine borders, being careful to turn trees as shown in photo. Sew one border to each side of the quilt. Sew an O patch to each outer edge of Tree blocks.

Taking It to the Finish

10 Sew the lining panels together. Follow the directions in the General Instructions for layering the lining, backing, and quilt top, and baste.

11 In each Sunshine block, quilt ¼″ inside the A patch. Quilt diagonal rays down the center of each C patch and extend across B.

In the outer borders, outline quilt around the vines and flowers. If you want to fill in the background more, quilt a diagonal grid 1″ apart as shown in the photo. Quilt ¼″ inside sashing strips and dark blue border.

Use bias binding to finish the edges, easing binding around the curve of O patches.

FULL-SIZE QUILT

1 If you want to make the full-size quilt, follow the instructions in Step 1 for the wall quilt and make 80 Sunshine block units.

2 Make 20 Sunshine blocks by following the directions in Step 2.

3 Join the Sunshine blocks in five rows of four blocks. Join the rows.

4 Make four Tree blocks as in Step 4 of the wall quilt assembly and set aside.

5 Prepare the long vines and stems for borders as described in the wall quilt instructions. Make four vines, two 90″ long and two 70″ long, and 16 stems.

6 Prepare the appliqué patches as described in Step 6 of the wall quilt assembly.

7 Use longer bias vines on long borders and shorter vines on short borders. Arrange the vine so that the curves are evenly spaced along the borders as shown in the diagram. Baste the

vines in place. Arrange stems, leaves, and flowers as shown; baste. Blindstitch appliqué patches.

8 Sew short dark blue borders to top and bottom of quilt. Sew long dark blue borders to sides.

9 Sew the outer borders to the quilt following the instructions for the wall quilt.

10 Sew the lining panels together. Layer the lining, batting, and quilt top, and baste. The quilting suggestions for the wall quilt will work beautifully here as well. Don't forget to make a label for your keepsake quilt.

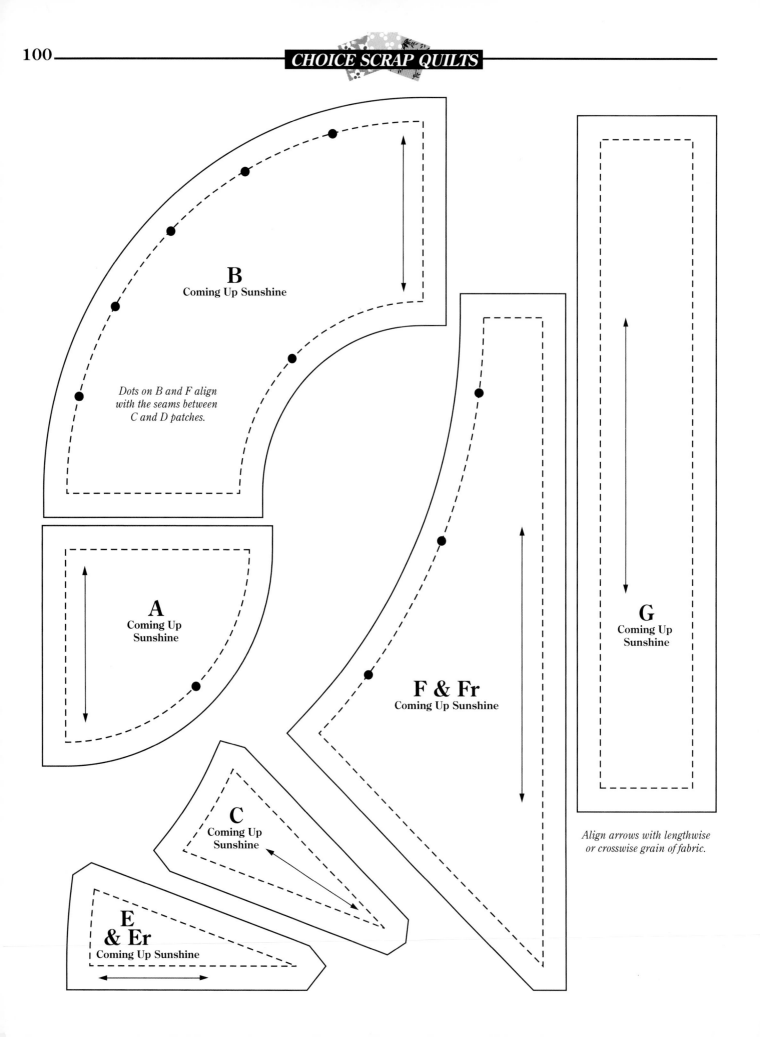

B
Coming Up Sunshine

Dots on B and F align with the seams between C and D patches.

A
Coming Up
Sunshine

F & Fr
Coming Up Sunshine

G
Coming Up
Sunshine

Align arrows with lengthwise or crosswise grain of fabric.

C
Coming Up
Sunshine

E
& Er
Coming Up Sunshine

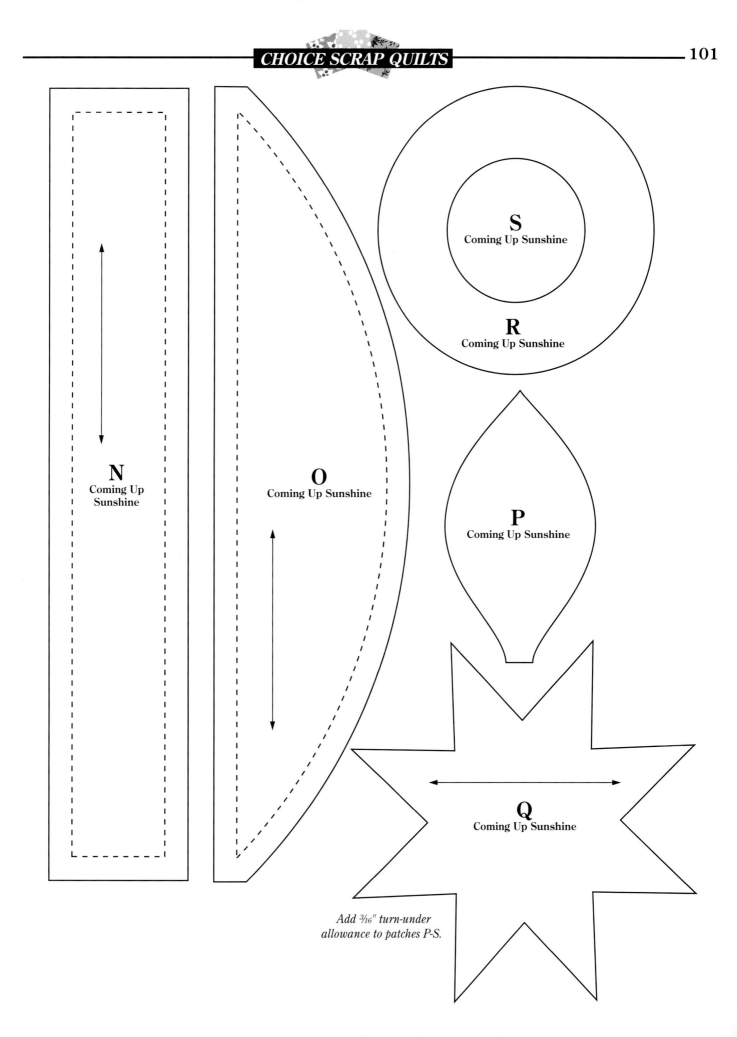

N
Coming Up
Sunshine

O
Coming Up Sunshine

S
Coming Up Sunshine

R
Coming Up Sunshine

P
Coming Up Sunshine

Q
Coming Up Sunshine

*Add ³⁄₁₆″ turn-under
allowance to patches P-S.*

Whirlwind

Designed by Judy Martin and made by Linda Holst

Wild geese whirl in all directions as though blown by the four winds in this pattern based on traditional old favorites such as Flying Geese, Wild Goose Chase, and Odd Fellows. We've taken hues from all over the spectrum and colored the same block many different ways. Each of the 25 blocks has a different arrangement of scraps placed so as to achieve different effects. Within some blocks, we've used some of the same fabrics in certain patches to emphasize the eight-pointed star within the block, while in other blocks our color choices make the flying geese more noticeable. You'll have so much fun experimenting with different effects!

FULL-SIZE QUILT

Making the Blocks

1 First, sort your scraps into lights, mediums, and darks. Organize a work space so you can use a large flat area for color experimentation when you begin to arrange the patches into blocks.

2 Cut patches as listed in the box. Look at the block drawing carefully and lay out the patches for one block at a time. Note that red solid C patches form the corners of each block to add symmetry to the overall design. Experiment with color placement, trying for different effects to emphasize different areas of the block. Join the patches as shown in the block piecing diagram. Repeat to make a total of 25 blocks, with each one different. Press each block.

Assembling the Quilt Top

3 Lay out the completed blocks on the floor or a large table to check placement for color balance. Move them around

as necessary until you are satisfied with the overall arrangement. Working one horizontal row at a time, join six sashes (F's) alternately with five blocks. Repeat for the other block rows. Join six setting squares (E's) alternately with five sashes to make a sash row. Repeat to make a total of six sash rows. Join block rows alternately with sash rows as in the quilt photograph. Press seam allowances toward sashes.

4 Add borders, mitering corners and trimming excess to leave ¼″ seam

allowances. Press the quilt top.

Taking It to the Finish

5 Mark the quilting motifs in A, B, and F patches. Sew the lining panels together. Assemble and baste the lining, batting, and quilt top. Quilt the marked patches. Outline quilt all other patches ¼″ from seams. Finish the quilt with double-fold binding.

WALL QUILT

1 Follow Steps 1 and 2 of the directions for the large version of Whirlwind, but make a total of 12 blocks.

2 Lay out blocks on the floor or a table to check placement for color balance; adjust as necessary. Working one row at a time, join four sashes (F's) alternately with three blocks. Repeat for the other block rows. Join four E setting squares and three sashes to made a sash row. Repeat to make five sash rows. Join block rows and sash rows alternately. Press seam allowances toward sashes. Add borders, mitering corners. Press quilt top.

3 Complete the quilt as explained in Step 5 for the full-size version.

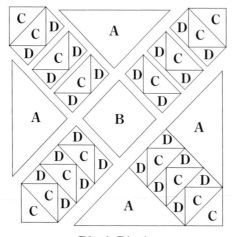

Block Piecing

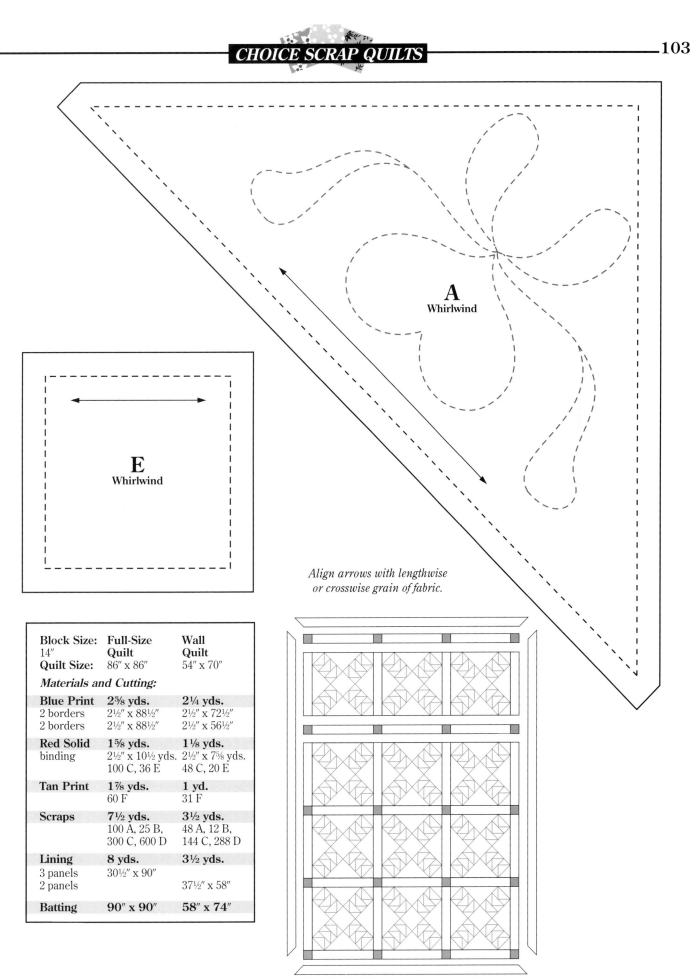

A
Whirlwind

*Align arrows with lengthwise
or crosswise grain of fabric.*

E
Whirlwind

Block Size: 14″	Full-Size Quilt	Wall Quilt
Quilt Size:	86″ x 86″	54″ x 70″

Materials and Cutting:

Blue Print	**2⅝ yds.**	**2¼ yds.**
2 borders	2½″ x 88½″	2½″ x 72½″
2 borders	2½″ x 88½″	2½″ x 56½″
Red Solid	**1⅝ yds.**	**1⅛ yds.**
binding	2½″ x 10½ yds.	2½″ x 7⅝ yds.
	100 C, 36 E	48 C, 20 E
Tan Print	**1⅞ yds.**	**1 yd.**
	60 F	31 F
Scraps	**7½ yds.**	**3½ yds.**
	100 A, 25 B,	48 A, 12 B,
	300 C, 600 D	144 C, 288 D
Lining	**8 yds.**	**3½ yds.**
3 panels	30½″ x 90″	
2 panels		37½″ x 58″
Batting	**90″ x 90″**	**58″ x 74″**

Wall Quilt Assembly

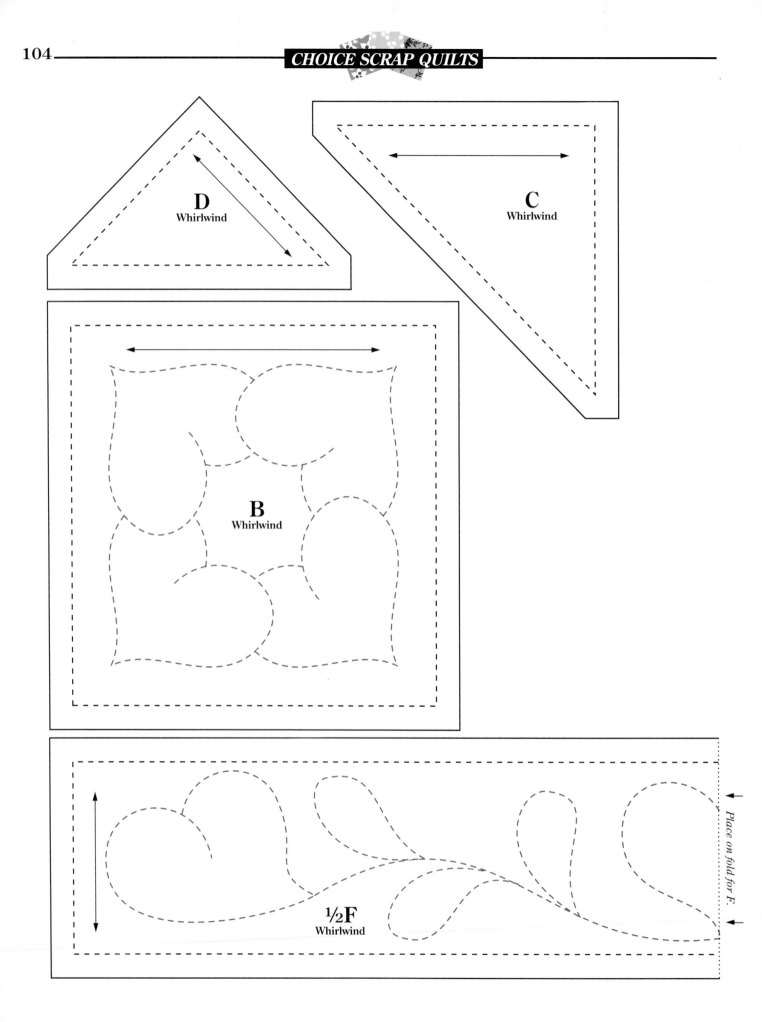

D
Whirlwind

C
Whirlwind

B
Whirlwind

½F
Whirlwind

Place on fold for F.

Give and Take

*Designed by Theresa Eisinger, made by
Carolee Miller and Maria Reardon Capp*

*It's fun to create a quilt that looks like
it is made from a difficult pattern for
advanced quilters only, but which actually is a breeze to put together. If you have
wanted to make one of these fool-the-eye
designs, Give and Take may be just the
pattern you're looking for. It uses only
one pattern piece in a variety of light,
medium, and dark prints, arranged in a
setting reminiscent of a Log Cabin, Barn
Raising style. You might even want to
consider making it as a charm quilt, a
style popular in the late 19th and early
20th centuries, in which every patch is a
different piece of fabric. We've used a
rainbow of colors in our version, but
choosing all your fabrics from one color
family would also make a pretty quilt.*

*We've supplied a pattern, but Give
and Take is also a prime candidate for
rotary cutting. For quick results, tie the
quilt as we did, or you can machine or
hand quilt if you prefer.*

FULL-SIZE QUILT

Making the Blocks

1 Prewash fabrics. Damp dry and press, then separate your scraps into lights, mediums, and darks. You will need only half as many light or dark patches as mediums, so add your medium-light and medium-dark fabrics to the pile of mediums. Read the General Instructions to find out how to prepare the templates and how to mark your fabric. Cut the patches you need as shown in the materials and cutting box or as described in the rotary cutting instructions.

2 The only difference between the X, Y, and Z blocks is the placement of the light, medium, and dark fabrics. It would help to keep the color values straight to sew all of the X blocks, then all of the Y's, and finally all the Z blocks. Make 84 X blocks, 44 Y blocks, and 40 Z blocks, using the block dia-grams for help. Be sure to keep the fin-ished blocks separated by type until you are ready to lay them out.

Assembling the Quilt

3 The quilt assembly diagram shows how to lay out the blocks in order, but you will need to look at the photo-graph to see how to turn them. Lay out the blocks in 14 rows of 12 blocks each, turning them whenever necessary to follow the design. First join the blocks in rows, then sew the rows together.

4 Fold all the border strips in half to find the centers, then finger-crease to mark the spot. Match the centers and sew the inner and outer *short* bor-der strips together, then match the centers and sew the inner and outer *long* border strips together. Match the center of each long border strip to the center of each side of the quilt top. Pin in place, with the red border on the inside, with raw edges matching. There will be extra length on each end of the border for mitering the corner. Stitch as pinned, starting and stopping ¼" from the seam edges. Add the short combined border strips to the top and bottom, using the same steps. You'll find directions for mitering the corners in the General Instructions. Miter the

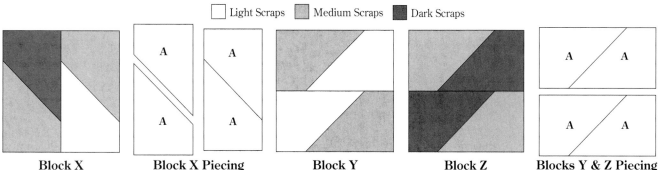

☐ Light Scraps   ▨ Medium Scraps   ■ Dark Scraps

Block X   **Block X Piecing**   **Block Y**   **Block Z**   **Blocks Y & Z Piecing**

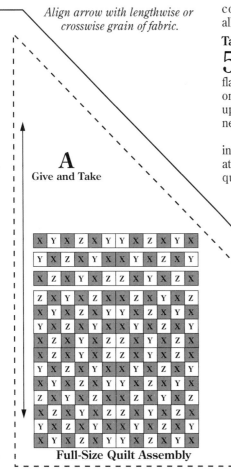

Align arrow with lengthwise or crosswise grain of fabric.

A
Give and Take

Full-Size Quilt Assembly

corners and trim the excess seam allowances to ¼″.

Taking It to the Finish

5 Sew the lining panels together. Place the lining right side down on a flat surface, then spread out the batting on top, and then the quilt top right side up. Baste the layers together, using a needle and thread or small safety pins.

To tie the quilt, follow the directions in the General Instructions, making ties at the corners of each block. For hand quilting, outline quilt ¼″ inside each shape and inside each border. After quilting or tying, apply double-fold binding.

WALL QUILT

1 Prepare fabrics and templates as listed in the first step of the full-size quilt assembly, then cut the patches needed for the wall quilt.

2 Make eight X blocks, four Y blocks, and four Z blocks. Using the wall quilt assembly diagram to help you, lay out the blocks in four rows of four each, turning as necessary. Join the blocks in rows, then sew the rows together.

3 Fold each border in half to find the center. Matching centers to the quilt top, stitch a border to each side, stopping and starting ¼″ from the edges. Miter corners and trim the excess seam allowances.

4 Finish the wall quilt, using the same method as in Step 5 of the full-size quilt above.

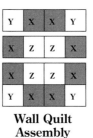

Wall Quilt Assembly

Wall Quilt

Block Size: 6″	Full-Size Quilt	Wall Quilt
Quilt Size:	81″ x 93″	27″ x 27″
Quilt Requires:	84 X Blocks	8 X Blocks
	44 Y Blocks	4 Y Blocks
	40 Z Blocks	4 Z Blocks

Materials and Cutting:

Lt. Scraps	**2⅛ yds.**	**¼ yd.**
	172 A	16 A
Med. Scraps	**4 yds.**	**⅜ yd.**
	336 A	32 A
Dk. Scraps	**2 yds.**	**¼ yd.**
	164 A	16 A
Red Print	**2⅝ yds.**	**¼ yd.**
2 borders	2″ x 89½″	2″ x 29½″
2 borders	2″ x 77½″	2″ x 29½″
Blue Print	**2⅞ yds.**	**⅓ yd.**
2 borders	3½″ x 95½″	
2 borders	3½″ x 83½″	
binding	2½″ x 10½ yds.	2½″ x 3¼ yds.
Lining	**7½ yds.**	**1 yd.**
3 panels	33″ x 85″	
1 panel		31″ x 31″
Batting	**85″ x 97″**	**31″ x 31″**

TIPS FOR ROTARY CUTTING

Make a template for patch A following the directions in the General Instructions.

Using your rotary cutter and ruler, cut your scraps into 3½″-wide strips. Each scrap must be at least 5½″ long, but can be much longer if you wish to use several patches from the same fabric. Stack four or more of the strips, all with the right side of fabric *up,* and square off one end. Place the template on the squared end of the stacked strips, and line up the ruler with the diagonal edge. Cut along the edge.

Rotate the template and line up the diagonal edge with the cut fabric, and cut the stack of fabric at the square end. Repeat this process until you reach the end of the strips. Be sure to trim the corner of each fabric patch to match the corner of the template.

If you are making a charm quilt, with every patch a different fabric, you can still use your rotary cutter. Stack up to eight fabrics, lining up the grain lines, and cut all four sides of the template using the ruler. Trim the fabric patch corners as needed.

Cutting along the diagonal

Cutting all four sides

Plaid Parade

Designed and made by Sissy Anderson

We named this quilt Plaid Parade because of the bold effect of the plaid scraps marching along in diagonal rows. However, its original name was "You're Right, Daddy, They Do Go Together." Its maker, Sissy Anderson, gave it that name because her father used to love to mix plaids in his clothing, despite his family's teasing. After he died, Sissy made this quilt from his clothes and realized that "You're right, Daddy, they do go together." Because plaids are sometimes not printed precisely on the grain of the fabric, the lines in the plaids may not align perfectly along the edges of the sewn patches. This adds a little movement and excitement to the overall design and contributes to the comfortable, homey feel of this quilt.

This pattern is easy to sew together, but be sure to turn the blocks as shown so the correct color arrangement is formed.

TWIN-SIZE QUILT

Making the Blocks

1 The number of patches you need to cut from each color is listed in the materials and cutting box. For each block, choose four A and two B from the cream scraps, and four A and two B from the plaid scraps. Arrange the plaid A's diagonally from corner to corner, and the plaid B's on the opposite corners, as we show in the block piecing diagram. Make 130 blocks.

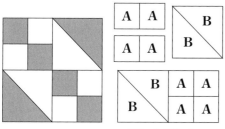

Block Piecing

Assembling the Quilt Top

2 Notice in the quilt photo that the blocks are rotated to form the pattern. Lay out your completed blocks on a flat surface to make sure you have them turned correctly. Rearrange the blocks until they are just the way you want them. Join the blocks in 13 rows of 10 blocks each. Press the seam allowances of alternating rows in opposite directions so that when rows are joined, the seams are butted. This makes it easy to align the blocks as you are stitching rows together. Join rows.

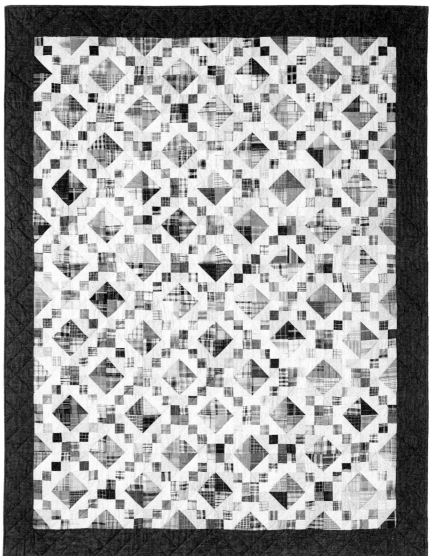

3 Fold the border strips in half to find the center of the long edges. Mark the center with a crease or a pin. Then fold the quilt top in half to find the center of each edge and mark it. Matching centers, sew the borders to the quilt, stopping the stitching ¼″ from the edge of the quilt. Miter the corners following directions in the General Instructions.

Taking It to the Finish

4 There are two options presented for quilting the border. If you choose the floral quilting motif, mark nine motifs in the short borders and 11 motifs in the long borders, spacing the motifs evenly.

Sew the lining panels together, pressing the seam open. Layer the quilt lining, wrong side up, with the batting and the quilt top. Baste the layers together. Quilt in-the-ditch around the patches. Quilt the borders you have marked or use masking tape aligned with the seams of the blocks to quilt diagonal lines as shown in the alternate border quilting. Apply double-fold binding to finish.

WALL QUILT

1 Follow the directions in Step 1 of the twin-size quilt assembly to cut and arrange the patches for the block. For this size, you need only 36 blocks.

2 Lay your blocks out on a flat surface to arrange them in six rows of six, rotating them to form the pattern. Stitch the rows together as you have arranged them.

3 If you are using the floral quilting motif in the border, mark five motifs along each border, spacing them evenly. Follow Steps 3 and 4 of the twin-size quilt assembly to finish your quilt. You can add a 3″-wide sleeve along the top back edge to hang the quilt with a rod.

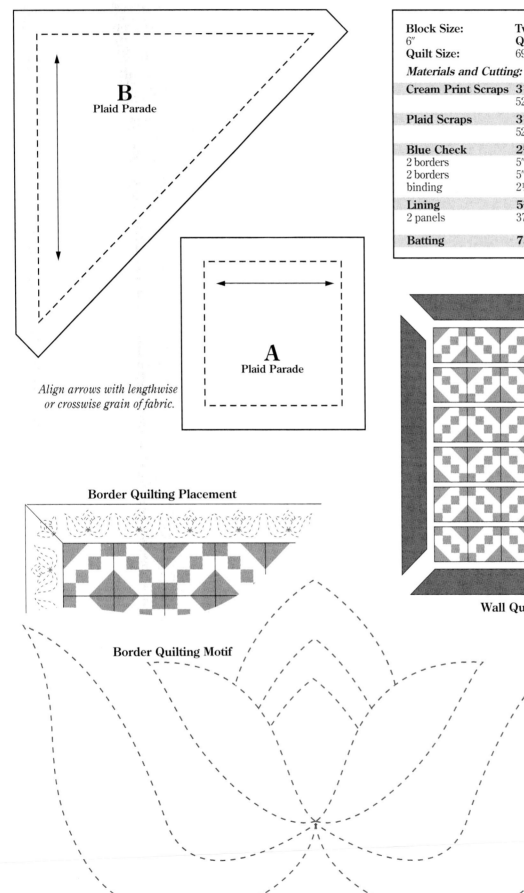

B
Plaid Parade

A
Plaid Parade

Align arrows with lengthwise or crosswise grain of fabric.

Block Size: 6"	Twin-Size Quilt	Wall Quilt
Quilt Size:	69" x 87"	45" x 45"
Materials and Cutting:		
Cream Print Scraps	3¼ yds.	1 yd.
	520 A, 260 B	144 A, 72 B
Plaid Scraps	3¼ yds.	1 yd.
	520 A, 260 B	144 A, 72 B
Blue Check	2⅝ yds.	1½ yds.
2 borders	5" x 89½"	5" x 47½"
2 borders	5" x 71½"	5" x 47½"
binding	2½" x 9⅜ yds.	2½" x 5½ yds.
Lining	5⅜ yds.	2⅞ yds.
2 panels	37" x 91"	25" x 49"
Batting	73" x 91"	49" x 49"

Wall Quilt Assembly

Border Quilting Placement

Border Quilting Motif

Alternate Border Quilting

More Blocks for Scrap Quilts

Making your very own scrap-quilt designs is easy and fun. In this section, we offer patterns for 15 12″ blocks that you can use singly or in combination to make a quilt the way you want it. To help you visualize your creation, you can make nine photocopies of each of your favorite blocks. Then cut out the individual paper blocks. Lay them side by side to see how they look together and what surprising secondary patterns form. Taking advantage of these secondary patterns can be quite excit-

ing. The blocks in this section can also be alternated with plain blocks or used with sashing for a totally different look.

Many blocks are more dynamic when placed in a diagonal setting, which requires the addition of side and corner triangles. For any diagonally set quilt using 12″ blocks, cut an 18¼″ square on both diagonals to make four side triangles. Cut as many of these as you need for your quilt. Cut two 9⅜″ squares in half diagonally for the corner triangles. As-

semble the quilt in diagonal rows, including the side triangles in each row. Sew the rows together and add the corner triangles last.

After you have decided on a setting for your photocopied blocks, you can fasten them to a sheet of paper, make copies of the sheet and try out various combinations of values (lights, mediums, and darks), using felt pens, colored pencils, or crayons. Suggestions for quilt sizes and settings are offered with each of the following blocks to get you started.

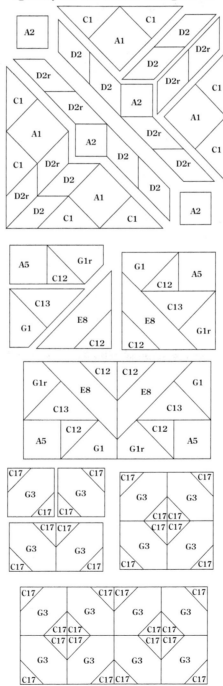

Galaxy...When these blocks are sewn together, a strong diagonal grid becomes apparent. As a variation, a secondary design of eight-pointed stars and four-patches is formed at the block intersections when alternate blocks are rotated one-quarter turn clockwise. See the figure. A setting 5 x 6 with a 5″ border makes a quilt 70″ x 82″.

Noon and Night...Like several other blocks in this collection, Noon and Night is made up of four 6″ units. These can be used separately as corner squares for any quilt with a corresponding 6″ border. Check your scrapbag for country color combinations such as cranberry, rose, and navy, or contemporary ones such as tangerine, yellow, and black. A king-size quilt can be made from 64 blocks set 8 x 8. Add a 6″ border for a finished size of 108″ x 108″.

Paths To Piece...This block makes a handsome diagonal grid pattern when set side by side. For a totally different look, reverse the light and dark scrap patches. Another possibility is to make the X's dark and the O's light in alternate rows, as in the figure. Use 42 blocks set 6 x 7 with a 3″ border for a 78″ x 90″ full-size quilt.

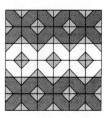

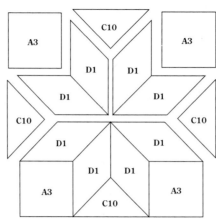

LeMoyne Star...As a suggestion, try using scraps in two color families, such as blue and green, and alternate them in adjacent diamonds. Alternating scraps of the same color but different values would also work well. Set 42 blocks 6 x 7 and add a 6″ border to make a quilt 84″ x 96″.

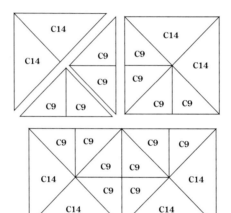

Peace and Plenty...Depending on your choice of light, medium, or dark scraps, you can emphasize the diamond-in-a-square aspect of this block, or you can make the pinwheel stand out. Thirty blocks, set 5 x 6, combined with 2″ sashing between the blocks, a 2″ inner border, and a 6″ outer border, will produce a quilt 84″ x 98″ for a full-size bed.

Hopscotch...Made from the classic Flying Geese pattern, this block provides a great way to use up your scraps. You might want to try assembling the quilt in groups of four blocks, each of which is rotated a quarter turn with sashing and setting squares in between. A quilt 79″ x 92½″ can be made of 30 blocks, set 5 x 6, with the addition of 1½″ sashing and setting squares, a 1½″ inner border, and a 5″ outer border.

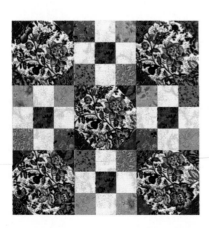

Delaware Flagstone...It would be fun to incorporate striped and plaid scraps in this block, alternating them in checkerboard fashion in the square patches. With the addition of animal or toy motifs in the octagonal patches, a quilt made from this block would be a wonderful gift for a child. For a crib-size quilt 44″ x 56″, sew together 12 blocks, set 3 x 4 and add a 4″ border.

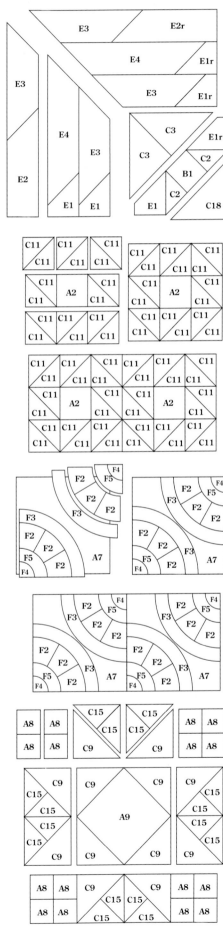

Pine Tree…Here's a chance to use your green scraps. To emphasize the individual trees, use a diagonal setting with 1½″ sashing. For Christmas, you can add a bright red stand (C18 patch) and embellish your trees with sequins, beads, and metallic thread or whatever you can find that strikes your fancy. For a full-size quilt, you will need 32 blocks (four across and five down), 14 side triangles, and four corner triangles. Add a 5″ border for a quilt 77⅞″ x 94⅞″.

Ribbon Quilt…Using scraps of the same color or value in the interwoven "ribbon" can accentuate the ribbon effect, or you can make the four pinwheels the focus of this block. To emphasize the pinwheel effect even more, make each one with scraps of a different color. Make a small wall quilt 36″ x 36″, before the border is sewn on, with nine blocks set 3 x 3.

Gypsy Trail…The fans in this block are pieced from your favorite scraps and then appliquéd onto the background squares. Changing the rotation of alternate units produces a pattern of little wagon wheels a child would love. Thirty blocks, set 5 x 6, will produce a quilt 68″ x 80″ with the addition of 4″ borders.

Use It All…Here is a pretty eight-pointed star to inspire you to dig into your stash of scraps. If you have many blue scraps, use those for the star and surround it with magenta or lavender, sparked with gold or black. Join 16 blocks, set 4 x 4, to make a wall quilt or a small quilt to snuggle under while you read or watch TV. If you add a 6″ border, the quilt will be 60″ x 60″.

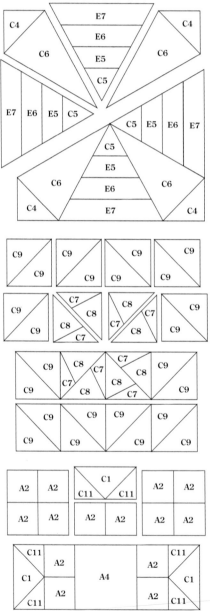

Building Blocks...This block lends itself to color gradations. Start with a color for which you have a lot of scraps and arrange them into light, medium, and dark. Don't worry if the gradations aren't exact; inconsistencies add to the liveliness of a quilt. Then use the scraps in order in the B2 patches, starting from the middle of the block. Choose a contrasting color for the center patch and fill in with complementary colors in the nine-patch units. In a 3 x 3 setting, nine blocks with a 3″ border will produce a small quilt 42″ x 42″.

Magic Pinwheel...Scraps in color gradations would be pretty in this block. Alternating light and dark scraps in the concentric squares also would be pleasing. As another suggestion, use the same color in all four C5 patches to form a square behind the pinwheel. Use a different color in each of the three remaining concentric squares. Forty-eight blocks set 6 x 8 and having a 5″ border make a queen-size quilt 82″ x 106″.

Missouri Windmills...Grace McKee, who designed this block in 1973, recommends that each windmill be a different color. To give the block a little pizzazz, try making each C8 patch (in the windmill only) in scraps of a bright print of one color and use dark or medium scraps of the same color for the C7 windmill patches. In a setting 5 x 7, 35 blocks with a 5″ border will make a quilt 70″ x 94″.

Maple Leaf...This pieced block has an appliquéd stem, but if you prefer, you can substitute another four-patch unit of A2 squares to match the other corners, changing the Maple Leaf to a star. Maple Leaf brings fall colors to mind: vermilion; magenta; ocher; rich, warm browns; and touches of lavender, but you could use fanciful colors as well: lemon yellow, fuchsia, sky blue, and purple. A full-size quilt 84″ x 96″ can be made from 42 blocks, set 6 x 7, with a 6″ border.

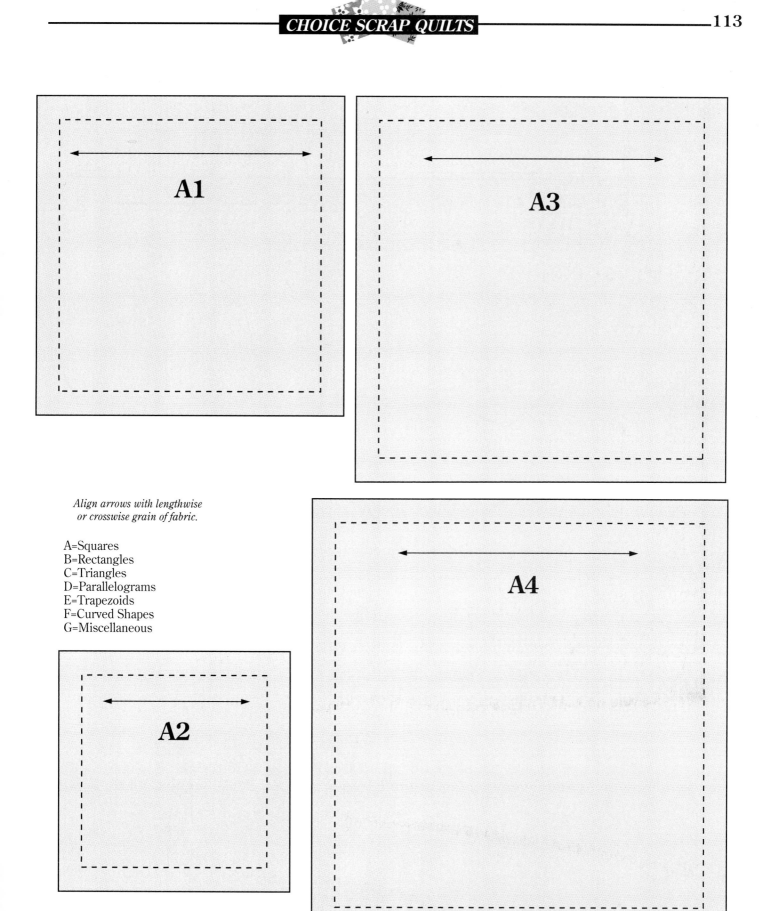

*Align arrows with lengthwise
or crosswise grain of fabric.*

A=Squares
B=Rectangles
C=Triangles
D=Parallelograms
E=Trapezoids
F=Curved Shapes
G=Miscellaneous

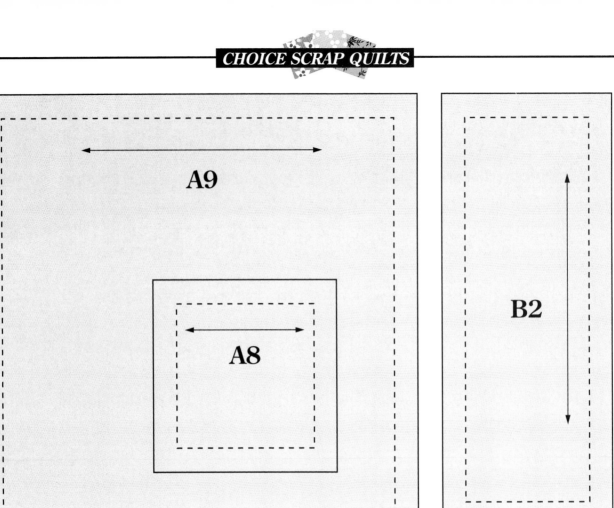

A9

A8

B2

*Cutting measurements
for A7 include
¼" seam allowances.
Finished size of A7 is 6".*

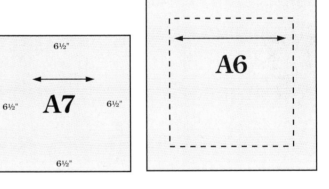

6½"

6½"   **A7**   6½"

6½"

A6

A5

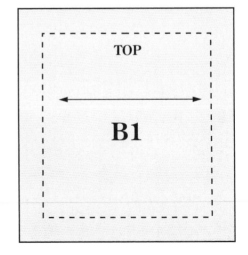

TOP

B1

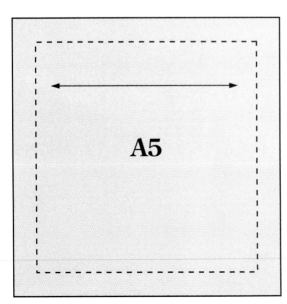

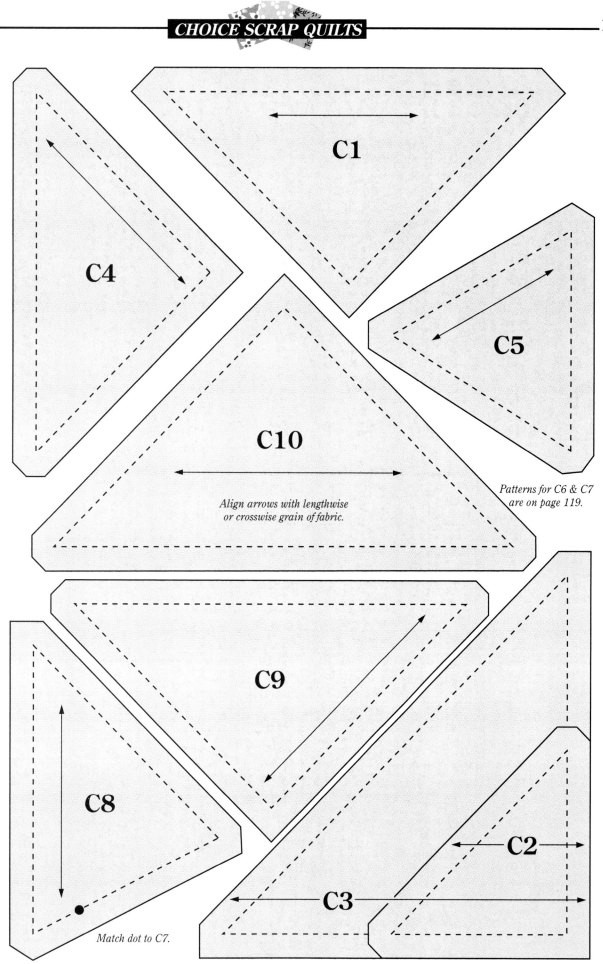

C1

C4

C5

C10

*Align arrows with lengthwise
or crosswise grain of fabric.*

*Patterns for C6 & C7
are on page 119.*

C9

C8

Match dot to C7.

C2

C3

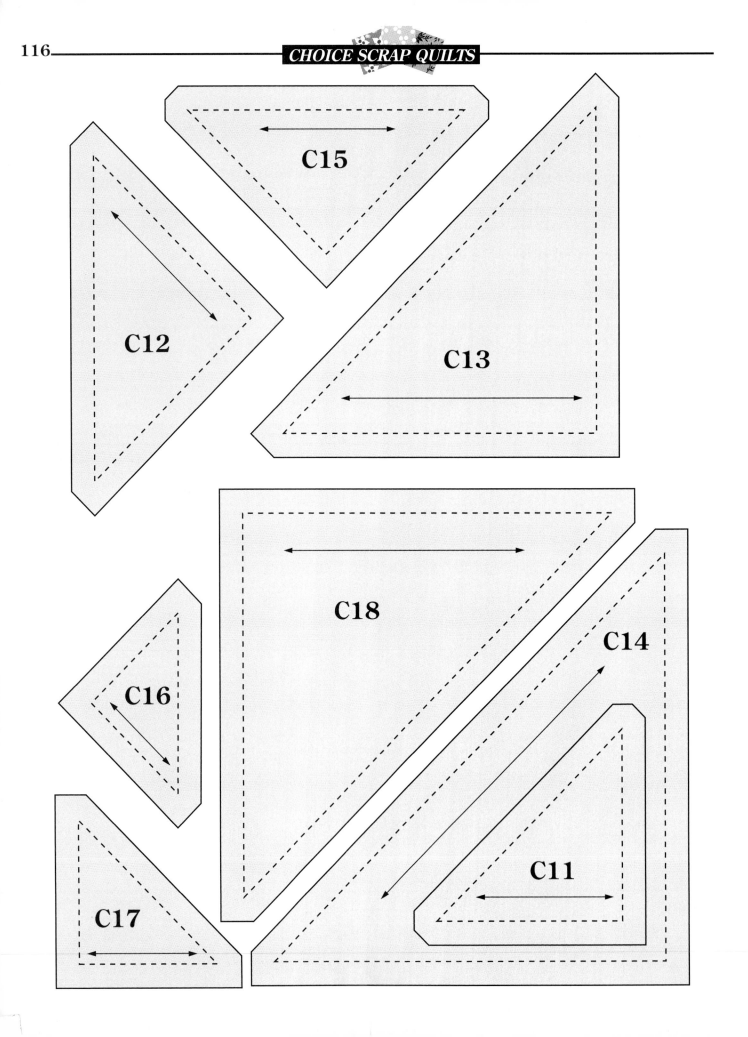

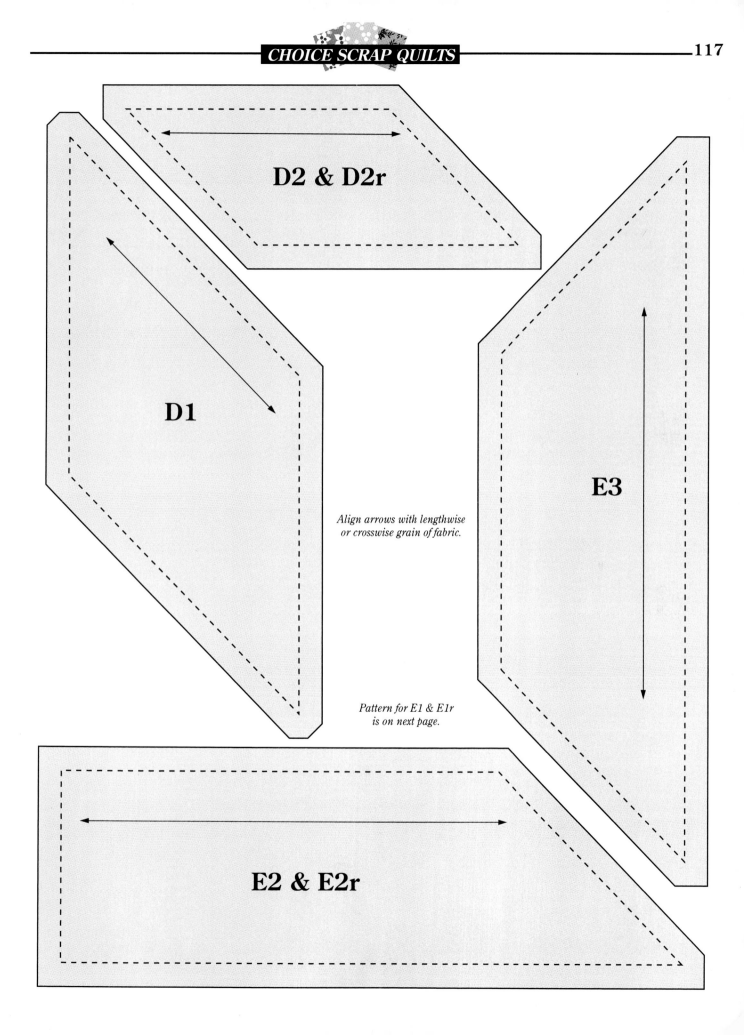

D2 & D2r

D1

E3

Align arrows with lengthwise
or crosswise grain of fabric.

Pattern for E1 & E1r
is on next page.

E2 & E2r

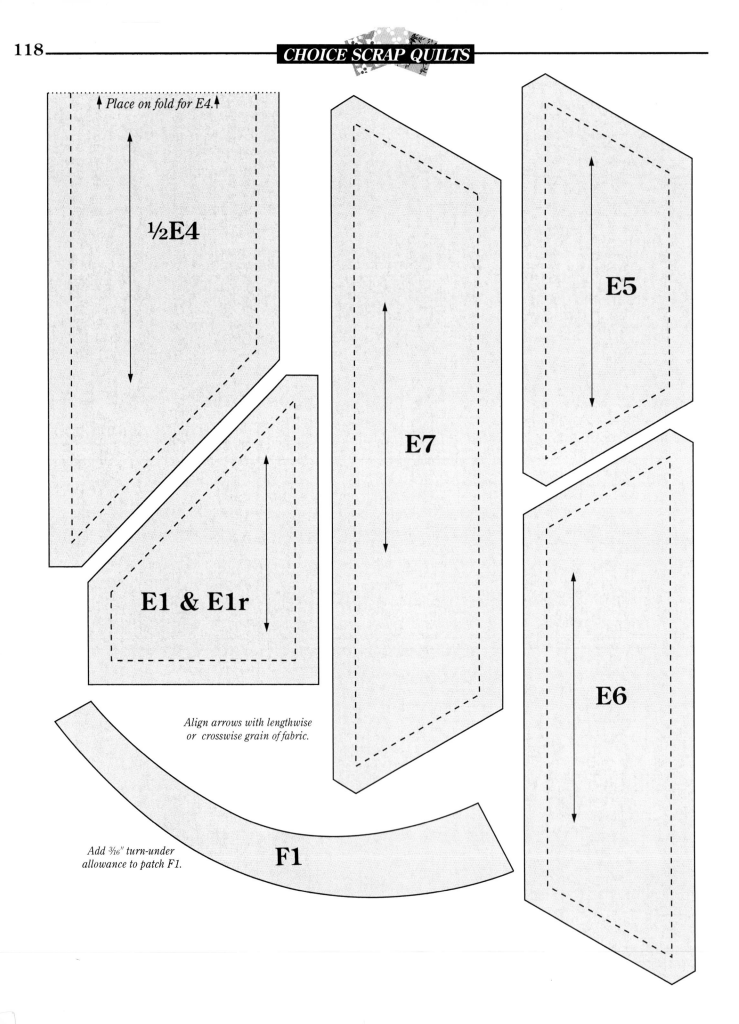

↑ *Place on fold for E4.*↑

½**E4**

E1 & E1r

E7

E5

E6

Align arrows with lengthwise or crosswise grain of fabric.

Add ³⁄₁₆" turn-under allowance to patch F1.

F1

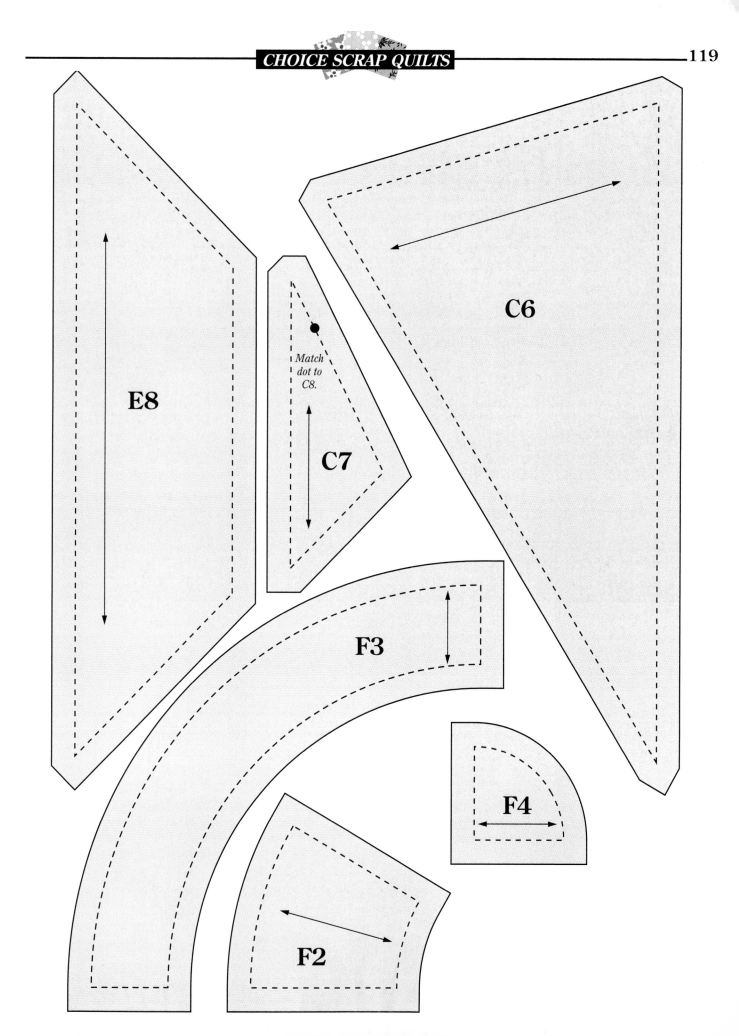

E8

C6

C7

Match
dot to
C8.

F3

F4

F2

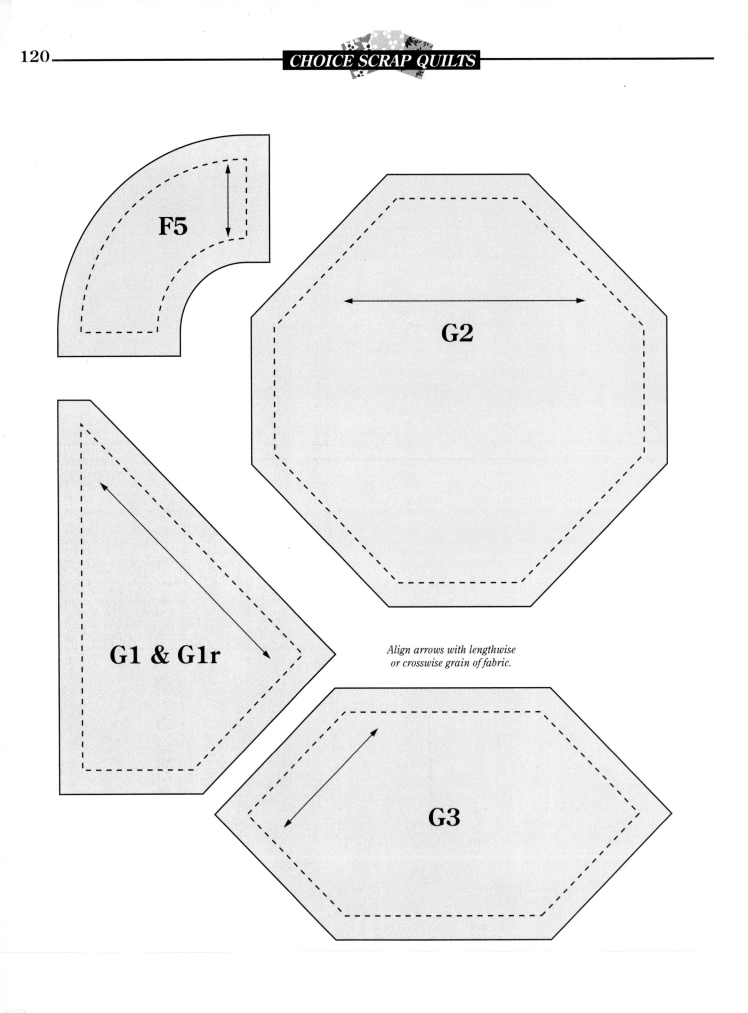

F5

G2

G1 & G1r

*Align arrows with lengthwise
or crosswise grain of fabric.*

G3